THE
CELTIC MYTHS

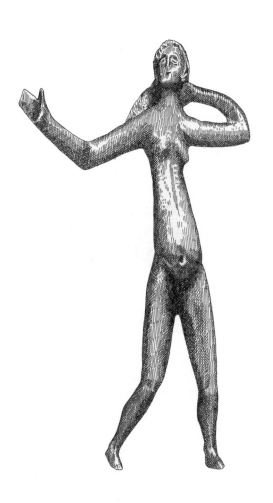

THE
CELTIC MYTHS
A GUIDE TO THE ANCIENT
GODS AND LEGENDS

MIRANDA ALDHOUSE-GREEN

WITH 82 ILLUSTRATIONS

Thames & Hudson

For Stephen
amoris causa

Acknowledgments

I am indebted to many people who helped make this book happen. To family and friends
who patiently endured my obsessive ramblings about myths, a huge thank you. I owe the
greatest debt of gratitude to the staff of Thames & Hudson, particularly Colin and Alice.
My three Burmese cats – Dido, Persephone and Taliesin – kept me company during the
long solitary hours of writing. The dedication of this book to Stephen is intended to
tell him how much I appreciate him and his unending support.

Half-title: Late Iron Age bronze figurine of a female dancer, from Neuvy-en-Sullias, France.
Frontispiece: Late Iron Age bronze boar, from Neuvy-en-Sullias, France.

First published in the United Kingdom in 2015 by
Thames & Hudson Ltd, 181A High Holborn, London WC1V 7QX

Reprinted 2018

The Celtic Myths © 2015 Thames & Hudson Ltd, London

British Library Cataloguing-in-Publication Data
A catalogue record for this book is available from the British Library
ISBN 978-0-500-25209-3

Printed and bound in China by Toppan Leefung Printing Ltd

To find out about all our publications, please visit **www.thamesandhudson.com**.
There you can subscribe to our e-newsletter, browse or
download our current catalogue, and buy any titles that are in print.

CONTENTS

Then Conchubar, the subtlest of all men,
Ranking his Druids round him ten by ten,
Spake thus: 'Cuchulain will dwell there and brood
For three days more in dreadful quietude,
And then arise, and raving slay us all,
Chaunt in his ear delusions magical,
That he may fight the horses of the sea.'
The Druids took them to their mystery,
And chaunted for three days.
FROM CUCHULAIN'S FIGHT WITH THE SEA, W. B. YEATS

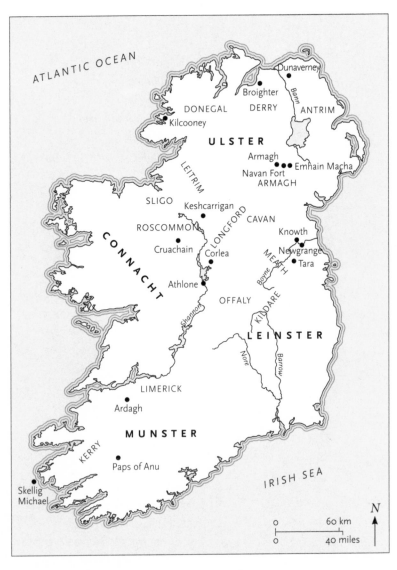

ATLANTIC OCEAN

Dunaverney

Broighter

DONEGAL DERRY ANTRIM

Kilcooney

ULSTER

Armagh Emhain Macha
Navan Fort
ARMAGH

LEITRIM

SLIGO Keshcarrigan

ROSCOMMON LONGFORD CAVAN

Knowth

C O N N A C H T Cruachain Corlea Newgrange
Tara

MEATH

Athlone

OFFALY

Boyne

KILDARE

LEINSTER

Nore Barrow

LIMERICK

Ardagh

MUNSTER

KERRY

Paps of Anu

IRISH SEA

Skellig
Michael

0   60 km
0   40 miles

N

Map of Ireland with regions and sites mentioned in the text

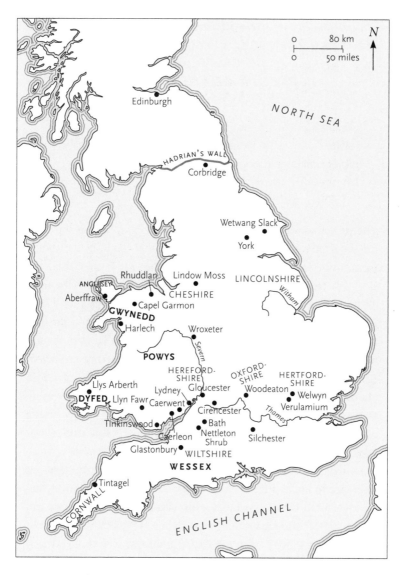

Map of England and Wales with regions and sites mentioned in the text

THE CELTIC WORLD:
SPACE, TIME AND EVIDENCE

*Gaul as a whole consists of three separate parts: one is
inhabited by the Belgae, another by the Aquitani and the
third by the people we call Gauls, though in their own
language they are called Celts.*
CAESAR, *DE BELLO GALLICO* 1.1

The principal focus of this book is the myths found in the early
medieval literature of Ireland and Wales that dates, in its written
form, to between the 8th and 14th centuries AD. It was with considerable trepidation that I embarked upon a book with the term
'Celtic' in the title. Since the early 1990s, archaeologists have seri-
ously questioned the use of the word to describe the ancient Iron
Age peoples of Western and Central Europe. Particular opprobrium
has been attached to the use of 'Celts' when referring to ancient
Britain. Whilst a plethora of authors from the Classical world
allude to the people of Gaul (roughly speaking France, Switzerland,
Germany west of the Rhine, parts of northern and eastern Iberia
and the far north of Italy) as being Celtic, no ancient author ever
spoke so of Britain. The Romans called the British *Britanni*.

A major issue that the anti-Celtic lobby has with the term, in
reference to ancient Europeans, is that it blurs the differences that
clearly existed between peoples with widely divergent cultures and
worldviews. It also means that some regions, such as the far north of
Europe, are excluded from the Celtic umbrella, even though many
cultural similarities between these areas and those further south can
be identified in archaeological evidence. Julius Caesar knew Gaul
intimately because he and his army were stationed there for nearly
ten years. The opening of his *De Bello Gallico* ('Concerning the

Gallic War') spoke of the now-famous division of the country into three major cultural groups: the Aquitani of the west, the Belgae in the east and the Celts who occupied the centre of Gaul. Caesar specifically stated that this last group identified themselves as Celts. This is important. For the most part, it is impossible to prove self-determination for prehistoric communities because they were non-literate and therefore written evidence of their own is absent. Even Caesar's use of the name Celts may have been nothing more than his presentation of a neat division that actually masked huge divergences within this group.

Despite the problems of knitting together ancient and early medieval identities, one important thing binds them together: language. Where there is evidence, for example from early and rare inscriptions or from place names recorded in Graeco-Roman geographies, it appears that the Celtic languages known and spoken today had their roots firmly in antiquity, for they are traceable in Gaulish, Celtiberian and old British words. It is true that language does not equate with ethnicity, but it does contribute powerful connective tissue. It is widely recognized, for example, that the use of the English tongue outside the United Kingdom carries with it a certain amount of cultural baggage, in spite of the yawning cultural gulfs between anglophone countries.

Names are essentially labels. Ancient Greece encompassed a series of city states – Athens, Sparta, Corinth and many more – united by a common language but regarding themselves as completely distinct. The Roman empire embraced a great swathe of the ancient world: from Britain to Arabia, people thought of themselves as belonging both to their indigenous communities and also to Rome. So, in the Biblical Acts of the Apostles, Paul of Tarsus confidently asserted that he was a *civis romanus*, a citizen of Rome, while at the same time he was a member of the wildly independent state of Judaea. So the question one can raise is this: is the use of the term Celtic any less legitimate *as a label* to describe peoples with certain important shared cultural elements than the term Greek or Roman? I think not.

Another issue to be considered is the origin of the term 'Celtic' as being used to describe the languages and peoples that we now take for granted as Celts: the Irish, Welsh, Scottish, Cornish, Manx, Bretons and Galícians. It was the 16th-century Classical scholar George Buchanan who first developed the notion of the Celts as a unified group of peoples living in Ireland and mainland Britain. So the concept of Celticity, as applied to Wales, Ireland and other regions on the western edge of Europe, is comparatively modern (in contrast with Caesar's use of the term in antiquity for those Celts he encountered on the Continent). Nonetheless, self-identity as a Celt is hugely important to the inhabitants of modern Celtic nations, such as Ireland and Wales. If people think of themselves as possessing a certain identity, that in itself gives credibility to that self-determination. For how else were identities created in the first place?

Where does this question of ethnicity leave the issue of Celtic mythology? In trying to establish connections between the cosmologies presented in the early pagan medieval literature and the earlier archaeological record of Iron Age and Roman-period Gaul and Britain, there is a major problem to be faced. The mythic texts belong principally to Wales and Ireland, whereas the bulk of archaeological evidence for 'Celtic' paganism is found in what is now England and the near-Continent. So there is some geographical disparity between the Iron Age and Roman evidence, on the one hand, and the home of Celtic mythic literature, on the other. But although medieval Gallic and British mythologies cognate with those of Wales and Ireland are largely missing, that is not to say that they did not once exist. Indeed, there are strong hints that shared cosmologies were once present. A prime example is the Coligny Calendar (see p. 174) from Central Gaul, written in Gallic and dating to the early part of the 1st millennium AD; it mentions the festival of Samonios, which has to be the same as the Irish New Year

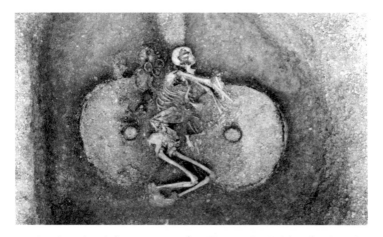

Iron Age chariot-burial of a young woman, from Wetwang, East Yorkshire, found in 1984.

celebration of Samhain. And there are many more that are explored in the following chapters. Nonetheless, the Celtic myths cannot be acknowledged as a window on the Iron Age. Research has proved categorically that Irish objects minutely described in the myths, such as Cú Chulainn's weapons and chariot, were of early medieval rather than prehistoric types.

Although this book is about mythic literature, these texts need to be placed in context, so, where relevant, it also contains backward glances at this earlier evidence provided by archaeology, and it strays eastwards beyond the borders of the Celtic West to consider possible origins of mythic characters and rituals in the ancient cultures of the *Britanni* and the *Galli*. The combination of literature and material culture provides a rich kaleidoscope of ancient beliefs and relationships between people and their gods on the western edges of the known world at a time when indigenous paganisms were confronting new religions. For the ancient Britons and Gauls, their Iron Age cults and practices had to adapt to and absorb the religious *mores* of Rome. Later on, it was Christianity that was Celtic paganism's greatest challenge.

Notes on Pronunciation

Don't be put off by the strange spellings of many Irish and Welsh names. Pronunciation can be a minefield, but here are a few examples that may help.

Pwyll	Pooilth
Matholwch	Matholooch (the ch is similar to Scottish 'loch'; emphasis is on the 2nd syllable)
Culhwch	Keelooch
Medbh	Mayve
Cú Chulainn	Coo Hulayn (emphasis on 1st syllable of 2nd word)
Oisin	Oysheen

One aspect of archaeological evidence not only serves to connect much of Iron Age Europe but also to reach forward into the early medieval period: art. Celtic (or La Tène) art had its genesis in the mid-1st millennium BC. Its rich and varied artistry, drawing on the natural world and the dream-wrought surrealism of the spiritual imagination, took many forms. Yet there is an overarching unity, in how artists and the consumers of their products perceived and expressed their world. Elements of such ways of seeing percolated down through time not only into early Christian art, as witnessed by decoration on Celtic crosses, for instance, but also into the medieval Celtic myths themselves. And so it is that magical heads, triple deities, enchanted cauldrons and half-human creatures are equally at home in Iron Age art and the later mythologies. As agents for the maintenance of these traditions through time, need we look further than the Druids, as time lords and curators of the past? Classical authors, such as Julius Caesar, speak of the Druids in Gaul and Britain as religious leaders and teachers, in whose keeping were the sacred oral traditions of the ancestors.

1

WORD OF MOUTH: MAKING MYTHS

*And after the mist, lo, every place was filled with light. And
when they looked the way they were wont before that to see
the flocks and the herds and the dwellings, no manner of thing
could they see: neither house nor beast nor smoke nor fire nor
man nor dwelling, but the houses of the court empty, desolate,
uninhabited, without man, without beast within them, their
very companions lost, without their knowing aught of them,
save they four only.*

FROM THE THIRD BRANCH OF THE *MABINOGI*

Myths, like fables, are elusive things. Modern horror films, whether
about vampires, ghosts or revived Egyptian mummies, are arguably
acceptable because they allow people to explore the darkest aspects
of human nature within a safe environment. In a sense, the same
is true of myth, but myths are much more complicated. This is
in part because they are almost always associated with religious
belief – and often magic – and also because contained in mythic
tales are answers to some of the most fundamental human concerns: Who are we? Why are we here? Why is our world like this?
How was the world created? What happens to us when we die?
Myths also explore issues related to initiation rites: birth, puberty,
marriage and death. Some, particularly those from the Celtic world,
are highly concerned with morality – good and evil, chastity, violence, rape and treachery, war and ethics – with gender-roles,
maidenhood, motherhood and virility; and with the ideals of female
and male behaviour.

Myths flourish in societies where such issues are not answer-
able by means of rational explanation. They are symbolic stories,
designed to explore these issues in a comprehensible manner. Myths

can serve to explain creation, natural phenomena and natural disasters (such as floods, drought and disease), the mysterious transitions of day and night, the celestial bodies and the seasons. They are often associated with the dreams and visions of so-called 'holy men', persons (of either gender) with the ability to see into the future and into the world of the supernatural. Myths are inhabited by gods and heroes, and tell of the relationship between the supernatural and material worlds. They can provide divine explanations for the departures of past peoples, their abandoned monuments and burial sites, their houses and places of communal assembly. Myths can explain the origin of enmities between

Trackways for the Spirits

No person had ever walked out on the bog but after that Eochaid commanded his steward to watch the effort they put forth in making the causeway. All the men made one mound of their clothes and Midir went up on that mound. Into the bottom of the causeway they kept pouring a forest with its trunks and its roots, Midir standing and urging on the host on every side.

FROM *THE WOOING OF ETAIN*

Wooden trackway across an Irish bog, built in 148 BC, at Corlea, Co. Longford.

communities and disputes over territory. Finally, myths are often highly entertaining tales that can while away a dark winter's evening by the fire.

• INTRODUCING THE WELSH AND IRISH MYTHS •

The main myths of Wales and Ireland are contained within medieval manuscripts that date between the 8th and 14th centuries AD, in their extant form. Three cycles of Irish prose stories comprise the principal surviving sources of Irish mythology. Earliest in its

Archaeological finds help connect the mythical cycles to their ancient origins. In the mid-2nd century BC a community at Corlea in Co. Longford, in central Ireland, constructed a great wooden causeway across a marsh to dry land. Tree-ring dating has established that the oak trees used for building this trackway were felled in 148 BC. Beneath the foundations a strange half-human, half animal image carved of ash was buried, perhaps as a foundation deposit, to bless the new road. The track may have been constructed in sections by different groups of people; certainly one section was never completed for there was at least one gap.

Certain Irish myths make references to the building of trackways across bogs. In the story of the divine Midhir and his love, Étain, Eochaid, king of Tar gave the god the 'impossible' task of constructing a wooden road across an impassable bog. Another tale relates a quarrel between two communities set to build a track across marshy ground from opposite ends, to meet in the middle. Having almost finished the job, the two groups fell out over its completion and it was never finished. Could this be the Corlea causeway? Could early Irish storytellers have woven into their narratives the remains of ancient roadways that were still visible in early medieval time?

Pages from the earliest manuscripts of Irish and Welsh myths. Left: from the Book of the Dun Cow, an 11th-century text containing the earliest known recension of the *Táin*. Right: from the Welsh Red Book of Hergest, one of the earliest compendia of the *Mabinogi*.

written form is the Ulster Cycle, whose focus is the epic tale of war between Ulster and Connacht, the *Táin Bó Cuailnge* (The Cattle Raid of Cooley), featuring the great Ulster hero Cú Chulainn and the dastardly Queen Medbh of Connacht. Historically, the province of Ulster had lost most of its political clout by the end of the 5th century AD. Its prominence in the *Táin Bó Cuailnge* argues for the Cycle's early origins. The first recension (copy) survives in fragments within the 11th-century Book of the Dun Cow, but the language used here belongs more properly to the 8th or 9th century. Another major source for the Ulster Cycle is the 11th-century Yellow Book of Lecan. The other two collections – the Mythological Cycle and the Fenian (or Fionn) Cycle – each survive in 12th-century versions. The first of these contains the most variety, and has vivid descriptions of pagan deities; the focus of the Fenian Cycle is the life of the eponymous Finn, heroic leader of a famous war-band and keeper of divine wisdom.

The Welsh myths are preserved in two principal collections of tales: the White Book of Rhydderch and the Red Book of Hergest. The White Book was put together in about 1300 and the Red Book in the later 14th century. The stories that are most rich in mythic content are the *Pedeir Ceinc y Mabinogi* (the Four Branches [sections] of the *Mabinogi*), known colloquially as the Mabinogion, and 'Culhwch and Olwen'. Other important material is contained within other tales, including 'Peredur', 'The Dream of Rhonabwy', and the fragmentary story 'The Spoils of Annwfn'. A further branch of myth deals at length with the heroic figure of King Arthur and the Quest for the Holy Grail. It is presented in the medieval French Arthurian Romances, whose best-known author was Chrétien de Troyes. Arthur makes several appearances in the Welsh myths too, particularly in 'Culhwch and Olwen' and 'Peredur', both of which are hero-tales.

• MYSTICAL VOICES: STORYTELLING FROM • ORAL PERFORMANCE TO WRITTEN WORD

Celtic myths had their genesis in early traditions of storytelling, of live performance. Just as musicians might travel from court to court to amuse the nobility, or skilled craftspeople to fulfil commissions for new armour or a decorative wine-cup, so poets and storytellers plied their trade. Many would have been peripatetic performers and in their travels they would have spread common stories from place to place. Others, like medieval court jesters, belonged to particular halls, and their tales would perhaps have more of a local flavour. But because the stories were held in people's heads, they would have grown and adapted organically, and no two tellings would have been exactly the same. So, for example, visiting storytellers might have woven features of the local landscape – mountains, rivers and

Oracle Stones

Pre-Christian stone sculptures from Ireland and Wales *may* represent the storyteller in action. They depict human heads, and on some their mouths are wide open as if in speech or song. A unique carving from Newry, Co. Armagh, is called the Tanderagee Idol. It is the image of a speaking man: his thick-lipped mouth gapes wide, and he appears to wear a horned headdress; the right hand is held diagonally across the body in the typical attitude of an orator, but it grasps something that may be a magical stone. It is tempting to interpret this image as a seer or shaman, wearing the animal-insignia that denotes his shape-shifting status, able to converse with the gods and propound their wisdom to his community. Traditional shamans often assume the persona of animals because they are

Iron Age stone figure known as the Tanderagee Idol, perhaps an image of an early Irish storyteller, from Co. Armagh.

trees – into their tales for the particular appreciation of local audiences. These mythic stories were alive, changed and grew with time and were embellished according to the skill of the narrator and the experiences of the community who listened to the tales.

> *'Our custom, lord,' said Gwydion, 'is that on the first night we come to a great man, the chief poet performs. I would be happy to tell a story.' Gwydion was the best storyteller in the world. And that night he entertained the court with amusing anecdotes and stories, until he was admired by everyone in the court, and Pryderi enjoyed conversing with him.*
>
> FROM THE FOURTH BRANCH OF THE *MABINOGI*

deemed to possess particularly close links with the Otherworld. So shamans frequently wear animal-skin cloaks or horns. The Tandaragee Idol has not been precisely dated, but it is likely to belong to the late Iron Age or early medieval period.

Wales has produced its own ancient 'oracle stones'. The Roman city of Caerwent in the southeast was the capital of the Silures, a tribe fiercely hostile to the Roman invasion of their territory in the mid-1st century AD. The town developed late and most of its public buildings date to the 4th century. Found at the bottom of a wealthy person's garden was a tiny shrine in which stood a carved sandstone head, its mouth wide open, again as if speaking or singing. It is easy to imagine visitors to the little sanctuary hearing the voice of the spirits through the medium of a magical speaking head.

Late Romano-British sandstone head from Caerwent, South Wales, with open mouth, perhaps an 'oracle stone'.

The Welsh word for a medieval storyteller was *cyfarwydd*, and its meaning is key to understanding the storyteller's role and status in society, for inside the word is a whole package of functions: guide, knowledgeable person, expert, perceptive one. The teller of tales was powerful, for he or she was a curator of tradition, wisdom and ancestral knowledge, all of which served to bind communities together and give depth and meaning to their world. It was not enough to be able to remember and recite a good yarn: stories needed to be carefully constructed and were heavy with significance.

Little is known about storytelling in action. However, just occasionally we are allowed a peep into the experience of the professional

teller of tales. It is especially rare for this to occur in the tales themselves, but the Fourth Branch of the *Mabinogi* provides us with a
glimpse into the experience of the *cyfarwydd*. The magician Gwydion
appears at the court of the Welsh lord Pryderi at Rhuddlan Teifi
(West Wales) and offers his services as a *cyfarwydd*. He spends the
evening entertaining the court and is declared to be the best storyteller ever known. He is fêted by all the courtiers, and especially by
Pryderi himself.

Medieval Welsh storytelling was close kin to poetry, and often
the poet and the *cyfarwydd* were one and the same. Of course,
modern audiences can only access the tales through their written
forms but, even so, their beginnings as orally transmitted tales are
sometimes betrayed by various tricks of the trade. Each episode is

---

Necessary Monsters: From Mythic Zoos to the Star Wars Bar

Then they became two warriors, gashing each other.
Then two phantoms, terrifying each other.
Then two dragons, pouring down snow on each other's land.
They dropped down then out of the air, and became two maggots.
One of them got into the spring of the river Cronn in Cuailnge, where
a cow belonging to Dáire mac Fiachna drank it up. The other got into the
well-spring Garad in Connacht, where a cow belonging to Medbh and Ailill
drank it. From them, in this way, sprang the two bulls, Finnbennach, the
white-horned, and the dark bull of Cuailnge.

FROM THE *TÁIN BÓ CUAILNGE*

The preface to the 1957 edition of Jorge Luis Borges' collection of essays
The Book of Imaginary Beings contains the comment that monsters
will always stalk mythic stories because real animals are a deeply
important part of human experience and because monstrous beings
are combinations of the real and the imagined, the stuff of nightmares
and dreams. The Classical mythic centaur, which melds the forms of
man and horse, has its Celtic counterpart in the Welsh horse-woman,

---

short and self-contained, as though to help listeners (and the storytellers themselves) remember them. Words and phrases are often repeated, again to aid memory. A third device also points in this direction, and that is the 'onomastic tag', the memory-hook provided by explanations of personal and place names. Then there is the use of number, usually 'three', which serves both as a magical number and as a way of constructing narrative to keep it in mind.

The Welsh stories are rich in dialogue, requiring different voices to play various roles in the narrative, from monsters to maidens, and from old sages to little boys, as well as a range of grunting and squeaking beasts. There are sonorous lists of names and possessions that demand to be declaimed aloud. There is poetry in the dialogue and in the repetition of questions within answers or of commands

Bronze figurine of a human-headed horse on a 4th-century BC wine-flagon from a grave at Reinheim, Germany.

Rhiannon. The Cretan Minotaur, a hideous blend of bull and human, can perhaps be seen transmuted in Irish mythology to become the great fighting bulls of Ulster and Connacht, which had human speech and understanding, or, in Wales, the enchanted boar Twrch Trwyth. Borges even goes so far as to argue that monsters are 'necessary' for human society. In our own day, fascinated by space and the possibility of worlds beyond, we conjure up fantastic images of galactic monsters, nowhere more clearly presented than in the *Star Wars* cantina, in which Skywalker and Solo encounter a collection of weird and wonderful beings from all over the Universe. Such are our modern mythic creations.

within acceptances, all of which once more serve to aid listening and remembering.

But what makes the Welsh and the Irish medieval stories something more than oral poetry, and turns them into myths, is the element of the supernatural and the presence of the gods. The Irish prose tales seem to be written versions of really old stories in which paganism was paramount and where the gods were omnipresent. Pagan pantheons are less obvious in the Welsh material and, indeed, there is frequent mention of the Christian God here. However, scrape away the surface and there lurks a rich tapestry of supernatural figures, deities, shamans and shape-shifters who certainly have no place in the Christian tradition.

• THE ART OF MYTH AND THE MYTH OF ART •

The evidence of artefacts helps us also bridge the gap between the assumed very early origin of these mythological cycles and their written forms. Because the early Continental and British Celts did not use writing, no mythic literature exists prior to the early medieval period. If we are to have any chance of recognizing that early myths were actually in circulation during the Iron Age and Roman period, the only place to trace them is in so-called 'narrative' iconography, containing multiple connected images that appear to tell a story. But even should it be possible to identify such artefacts, it is impossible to do more than hazard a guess as to possible meanings.

Glance at any book about Celtic art and you will find a fabulous array of imaginary creatures, all of which are based on the natural world but treated in a manner that in the 20th century would have been called surreal. Snakes have rams' horns, people have three faces, bulls have three horns, horses have human heads, men wear the antlers of alpha-male stags, and the human head is the paramount image.

Celtic art had its heyday between the 5th and 1st centuries BC, but on the western and northern fringes of Britain it continued to flourish long into the Roman era, until at least the 2nd century AD. In Ireland, where there was virtually no interruption by the ingress of Roman cultural traditions, native artistic styles survived the introduction of Christianity. The high Christian Insular art expressed in the illuminated manuscripts and stone crosses of the early Middle Ages includes depictions straight from the mythic repertoire of the pagan past: the number three, the human head and weird hybrid creatures. This means, of course, that the latest strand of Irish Celtic art co-existed with the birth of mythic literature.

• MYTHICAL MOTIFS •

Storytelling is the craft of speaking narrative. Certain devices or recurring themes were used in Celtic mythic tales, and as we explore them further, patterns and motifs will emerge time and again. These elements not only mark the stories out as having roots in an oral tradition of myth-making, but also show important concerns of the societies in which they lived. Crucially, many of these motifs found in the myths are also witnessed by the physical evidence from archaeology, as the three examples below show.

The Enchanted Cauldron

I was hunting in Ireland one day, on top of a mound overlooking a lake that was in Ireland, and it was called the Lake of the Cauldron. And I beheld a big man with yellow-red hair coming from the lake with a cauldron on his back. Moreover he was a monstrous man, big and the evil look of a brigand about him, and a woman following after him. And if he was big, twice as big as he was the woman; and they came towards me and greeted me. 'This woman', said he, 'at the end

*of a month and a fortnight, will conceive, and the son who will
then be born of that wombful at the end of the month and the
fortnight will be a fighting man full armed.'*

FROM THE SECOND BRANCH OF THE *MABINOGI*

A persistent feature of both Irish and Welsh mythology is the theme
of the magical cauldron, a vessel capable of raising the dead and
of providing ever-replenishing supplies of food. The Irish god
Daghdha, ('the Good God'), possessed a huge inexhaustible cauldron (see p. 182). The central focus of the Irish Otherworld feast
was the cauldron, which never ran out of food (see p. 101). One Irish
cauldron-myth was associated with sacral kingship, where the new
king of Ulster had to bathe in one, while consuming the meat and
broth of a white mare he had ritually 'married'.

The cauldron-myths span both sides of the 'Celtic pond'. In the
Second Branch of the *Mabinogi*, the heroine Branwen's brother
gives her husband a supernatural, life-regenerating cauldron and
the Irish king responds by admitting his prior knowledge of the
vessel, relating how its origins were actually Irish. It is clear from
the story that the vessel emanated from the Otherworld (see quote
above) and its association with reincarnation, like the Daghdha's
cauldron, supports this.

Many cauldrons have been found in Ireland, Scotland and
Wales, placed in a bog or lake as a ritual event, seemingly as a result
of beliefs about the connection between cauldrons and water. As
early as 700 BC, two beautifully made sheet-bronze cauldrons were
deposited, with other artefacts, in a remote lake called Llyn Fawr
(see also p. 184) in South Wales, probably a shrine visited by pilgrims
from far and wide. The affinity between cauldrons and water may
have had its beginnings in the life-giving and regenerative powers of
both natural watery places and liquid-holding vessels.

The Gundestrup Cauldron, made in the 1st century BC, is the
most spectacular Iron Age vessel so far found. It is particularly

Ceridwen's Cauldron

A Welsh mythic tale, preserved in a 13th-century text, The Book of
Taliesin, contains a rich story of an enchanted cauldron, whose contents
endowed those who ate or drank from it with knowledge and inspiration.
The cauldron's keeper was Ceridwen. She bore two children, Crearwy
('the light or beautiful one') and Afagddu ('black' or 'ugly'). Wanting to
compensate her son for his ill-favoured appearance, his mother mixed
a special brew in the cauldron, designed to give him absolute wisdom.
Because the potion needed to boil for a year, Ceridwen appointed a
young boy, Gwion, to watch over it. As he was tending the cauldron,
three drops of scalding liquid splashed onto his hand and, without
thinking, he licked his fingers, thus inadvertently acquiring the wisdom
intended for Afagddu. Gwion's flight and pursuit by the angry Ceridwen
eventually caused Gwion's rebirth as the great visionary poet Taliesin.

interesting as a very likely candidate for the expression of narrative myth. Its images record complex and interconnected narrative
scenes. The cauldron was found in central Jutland in 1891. Made of
gilded sheet-silver plates, heavily decorated with embossed images,
it was capable of holding 130 litres (34⅓ gallons) of liquid. It is
unique in terms of archaeological discoveries; it was clearly very
precious, and the nature of its ornamentation proclaims it as a
sacred vessel, used in the highest ritual contexts. It was constructed
of seven outer and five inner plates, plus a base-plate. The cauldron
was found deliberately dismantled into its constituent parts, neatly
stacked and buried deep in a remote peat bog.

The larger inner plates each depict a complex scene. On the
first, a Celtic army marches into battle, the dead being reborn by
being dunked in a vat by a supernatural being, all watched over by
a ram-horned snake, its hybrid nature perhaps reflecting a role of
mediator between worlds. A second scene depicts an antlered deity
as lord of the animals, accompanied by several beasts, including a

Gilded silver cauldron, depicting deities and mythological scenes, found on a dry island
in a bog at Gundestrup in Jutland, Denmark; 1st century BC.

stag and a second ram-horned serpent. The third shows a sky-god
with his solar wheel, with various weird animals including hyaena/
leopards, others with four feet, long curved beaks and wings, and
yet another ram-horned snake. The fourth plate bears triple images
of a sacred hunt, with three wild bulls about to be killed, perhaps in
sacrificial rituals; and the fifth depicts a goddess in a chariot flanked
by other dream-animals, including two very strange elephant-like
creatures with leopard-spots, and more winged, beaked beasts.

The seven outer plates contain less complex imagery. Whilst the
larger inner panels appear to depict narrative scenes or ritual events,
these seem to focus more on visualizing a Celtic pantheon, a rich
parade of gods and goddesses, all of whose individuality is represented by different attributes and hair/beard styles. Unlike the active
inner scenes, these outer images are portraits; they stare statically
out at the spectator, and are accompanied by smaller human and
animal figures. The base-plate is different again: its central feature
is a great dying bull, probably a wild aurochs, killed or sacrificed by
a hunter or priest.

Base-plate of the Gundestrup Cauldron. It depicts a dying bull being attacked by a diminutive human figure, perhaps a sacrificial offering.

The Gundestrup Cauldron appears both to narrate a myth and to present a panoply of divine beings. We can only guess at their meanings and at the association between one plate and another. It is clear that certain recurrent motifs were designed to exhibit connections: of these, perhaps the most telling is the ram-horned snake, which occurs on three inner plates. This image, like that of the antlered human figure, is by no means confined to the Danish vessel, but appears widely on indigenous Gallo-British sculptures dating to the Roman period, hinting at a fragmented group of cosmic stories that survived in limited form right through the period of Roman occupation in Britain, Gaul and the Rhineland.

How might the images on the Gundestrup Cauldron have worked in the context of storytelling? In a similar way, perhaps, to the manner in which myth-decorated scenes on ancient Greek pots may have acted as a focus of attention at *symposia* (drinking clubs), we can imagine the cauldron's function as a bard's 'prop', at the centre of a group clustered around the hearth-fire. In the flickering flames, the relief-pictures would glow and seem to move, and

the storyteller would give the cauldron its own voice. The dying bull on the base-plate would contribute an especially dramatic touch, for the animal's head had two holes, for the insertion of detachable horns (perhaps real ones) that would have jutted out of any liquid (blood or wine, maybe), in a visual myth of sacrifice and rebirth.

The Power of Three

> *Cú Chulainn reached Forgall's rampart and gave his salmon-leap across the three enclosures to the middle of the fort. In the inner enclosure he dealt three strokes at three groups of nine men. He killed eight men at each stroke and left one man standing in the middle of each group. They were Emer's three brothers, Scibar and Ibor and Cat.*
>
> FROM THE *TÁIN BÓ CUAILNGE*

Another persistent allusion is to triadism, or 'threeness'. Three seems to have been a sacred number in both Irish and Welsh tradition. In Irish mythic legends, the battle-goddesses variously called the Morrigna (singular Morrigán), the Badbh and Macha occur (like the witches in Shakespeare's *Macbeth*) in triple form. In the Irish pantheon, there were three craft-deities: Goibhniu, Luchta and Creidhne. The personification of Ireland itself was also presented as three goddesses: Ériu, Fódla and Banbha. The Ulster hero Cú Chulainn wore his hair in three braids and killed his enemies in threes. In stories relating to the killing of kings, this was done in three ways: by wounding, burning and drowning. Triplism is likewise found in Welsh mythic tales: in the Second Branch of the *Mabinogi*, Branwen is described as one of the three chief maidens of Britain; in the same tale, the dying Brân speaks to his followers of the three magical singing birds of Rhiannon. In the Fourth Branch, the magician Gwydion lays three curses on his treacherous brother Gilfaethwy so that his three sons are turned into three wild animals: a wolf, a deer and a boar.

Like the cauldron, the theme of 'three' as a special number is prominent in the cosmology of Britain and Ireland in the Iron Age and Roman periods. Triple heads were carved in stone: the Irish one from Corleck, Co. Cavan, consists of a circular stone with three faces sharing a 'skull', and a sculpture from the Romano-British town of Wroxeter in Shropshire depicts three identical conjoined heads. The tradition of triple-faced divinities is by no means confined to Ireland and Britain but is particularly common in Gaul, especially in Burgundy and at Rheims, tribal capital of the Remi. As well as triple-headed beings, gods recurrently appear in threes: in Roman Britain, triple 'mother-goddesses' are widespread, as are sculptures of three strange hooded figures known as *Genii Cucullati* (the 'hooded gods').

Stone relief of three goddesses from Corinium (Cirencester).

The 'Seeing Stone' of Corleck

At Corleck in Co. Cavan, a stone-carver, who probably lived sometime between the 4th and 1st centuries BC, took a stone and fashioned it into a human head. This was not a conventional portrait of a person or even of a god, but a highly symbolic object. For the sculptor had carefully carved three identical faces around the surface of the stone. Each pair of eyes looks in a different direction, as if scanning in front, behind and to one side. Why was the number three so significant to the maker of the head and to those for whom it was made?

Iron Age stone triple-faced head from Corleck, Co. Cavan, Ireland.

The Corleck head had never been part of a statue; it was designed to be an image of a disembodied head. Other three-faced heads are known from England and Scotland, so the Corleck stone-mason was not working in a vacuum, but according to a tradition shared over long distances. The dual symbolism of the head itself and its triple face contributed to an Iron Age cosmological code, in which sacred power was both expressed and enabled by the production and use of this highly charged object. It might depict a deity but it might equally have been used almost like one of Tolkien's *palantiri* or 'seeing stones' (used to gain knowledge of places or events far away in time or space), giving immense predictive magical potency to those holy people who could 'read' it and interpret its messages.

The particular significance of threeness to Celtic myth can only be assumed, but its common appearance in the archaeological record for the period before the myths were compiled in writing suggests that the later myths involving triadism borrowed some elements from earlier periods. In the Irish stories of triple goddesses, such as the Morrigán, it is clear that only one real persona or identity existed, despite the sometimes triple manifestation. The meaning behind triplism is more than mere emphasis because the number three is so specific and so favoured over other numbers. It was a holy number, charged with meaning and magic, and may have its genesis in such ideas as the presentation of past, present and future or, like the triple-layered cosmos of many 'modern' shamanistic traditions, it may have represented the upper-, middle- and underworlds.

Talking Heads

Conall Cernach was one of the supernatural heroes who features in the Ulster Cycle prose tale, the *Táin Bó Cuailnge*. He was a great warrior against Connacht and its leader, Queen Medbh, and he was decapitated in battle. But his severed head was so large that it could contain four adults, four calves or two people in a litter. Conall's hollowed-out skull clearly possessed similar powers to the cauldron of plenty, for the Ulstermen who drank milk from it regained their strength after they had been weakened by a curse. Conall had other associations with heads: he had a (surely rather uncomfortable) habit of sleeping each night with the severed head of an enemy Connachtman beneath his knee.

The final episode in the Second Branch of the *Mabinogi* describes the death of Branwen's brother, the hero Brân. He was killed with a poisoned Irish spear through his foot (reminiscent of what befell the Greek hero Achilles at the hand of Paris at the end of the Trojan War) during the great conflict between Ireland and Wales. Before he died, he gave his followers the curious instruction to cut off his head and take it to the White Mount in London, where it should be buried facing towards France, so that it could protect Britain from invasion from the Continent. Furthermore, he told his men that the head would not decay after being severed from his dead body but would be as good a companion to them as it had ever been to its owner until it was finally interred.

These are just two of many myths associated with human heads and their supernatural powers. As is perhaps true for cauldrons, the theme of supernatural disembodied human heads may have its roots in prehistoric ritual and belief. Peoples in Iron Age Ireland, Britain and Europe appear to have accorded the human head special reverence. Archaeological evidence provides clues as to how such veneration was expressed: by carving images of heads in stone and wood; by including head-symbols on decorated Iron Age metal-work and by repeatedly depositing real human heads in special places: wells, rivers, pits and temples.

Prohibitions and Curses

These will be your injunctions. You are not to go righthandwise round Tara and lefthandwise around Brega. You are not to chase the wild beasts of Cernae. You are not to go out of Tara every ninth night. You are not to spend a night in a house where firelight, which can be detected from outside, is seen after sunset.'
FROM NEMGLAN'S INJUNCTIONS ON KING CONAIRE MÓR,
IN 'DA DERGA'S HOSTEL'

The medieval Irish mythic tale known as the *Táin Bó Cuailnge* contains an account of Queen Medbh's bards and satirists whom she sent to attack a noble Ulsterman called Fer Diad. The weapons used were words and they could literally sandblast a man's face, raising boils and rashes. The power of words to wound was a recurrent bardic theme in medieval Ireland; it can be found as late as the 15th century, when a poem was written that recorded the threatened

Part of an Iron Age lead curse tablet from Larzac, Southern France.

infliction of just such an injury by a poet against a man who had burned his corn. The glowing wheatfields are likened to the scorched face of the arsonist, but the poet may have been influenced, at least in part, by Christian ethics of forgiveness, for he never actually carried out the punishment.

Curses are a common feature in Irish mythology. Called *gessa*, they are more properly described as prohibitions, warnings not to do something. It was the failure to heed the message that caused the curse to be fulfilled. We shall encounter just such a *geis* laid upon the Ulster hero Cú Chulainn (see pp. 105–112). Another tale has a series of *gessa* at its heart: 'Da Derga's Hostel' recounts how an Ulster king named Conaire Mor was burdened with a whole raft of prohibitions, the most serious of which was an injunction never to kill birds. This particular order was due to the manner of his conception and birth, the prediction of which was signalled by the appearance of a bird in his mother's house. Apart from the bird-curse, Conaire's *gessa* were closely related to his kingship, and many of them were designed to set boundaries for royal power. So, for instance, they limited his capacity to spend time away from his land,

and included a command not to allow his men to carry out raids. But it was Conaire's failure to keep faith with the initial bird-killing prohibition that led to his death (see p. 106).

Gessa fulfilled an important role for the storyteller, for their introduction at the beginning of a tale led to the anticipation that something awful would happen to the bearer of the *geis*. So *gessa* acted as a device to keep listeners interested, and one can imagine how, perhaps, a storyteller would break off his tale at a crucial moment, leaving his audience to wonder how it would end, avid for the next episode in the 'soap opera'.

• SCARY TALES OF THE SUPERNATURAL •

Some Celtic mythic tales are chilling to read even now and must have had even more frightening dramatic effects when told in hushed sepulchral tones to an audience sitting in the dark, with only the eerily flickering fire for comfort. Part of the Irish tale of 'Da Derga's Hostel' describes a nightmare vision of an infernal goddess. The very name of the story prepares its listeners: Da Derga means the 'red god', and red was the colour of the Otherworld. The hostel, or *bruidhen*, was an Otherworld dwelling, and the whole myth is based upon the killing of King Conaire, when he ventured, as a living being, into the realms of the spirits – always a perilous thing to do. The story of the luckless Conaire is doom-ridden from the start, and the audience would have known this. He was killed because he broke his bird-*geis* and – significantly – this took place at the end-of-year festival of Samhain, the pagan Irish equivalent of Hallowe'en, at the end of October. Samhain was an especially dangerous time because it took place at the interface between the end of one year and the beginning of the next, a time of 'not being' when the world turned upside-down and the spirits roamed the earth among living humans.

In his description of the hideous visitor to the hostel, the story-teller of 'Da Derga's Hostel' made the most of his licence to create the weirdest nightmare-ridden imaginings that he could devise: she was the goddess of death in the guise of an old woman, a noose around her neck, wearing a striped cloak. She had long black legs, a knee-length beard and her mouth was at the side of her head. She made prophetic utterances while standing on one foot. She came to the hostel just after sunset. This is heavy with symbolism that must have been well known to those listening, for all the imagery speaks of the unstable and monstrous Otherworld: the gender-crossing nature of the hag; her twisted features; her night-black limbs; her one-footed stance; and her bi-coloured mantle, all redolent of a being able to transgress between the layers of the cosmos. She appeared at the juxtaposition of day and night, the old year's end and the new year's birth, thus augmenting the threshold symbolism even further. Piling image upon image, the storyteller saturated his audience with the message of menace, of the unnatural mingling of humans and spirits, and built upon their anticipation of a grisly climax to the tale. They were not to be disappointed. Conaire was beheaded for failing to keep his bird-*geis*, but even then the supernatural flavour of the story continued, for his decapitated head spoke in praise of the man who had slain his killers.

2

THE MYTH-SPINNERS

*It is said that during their training, the Druids learn by heart
a great many verses, so many that some people spend 20 years
studying the doctrine. They do not think it right to commit
their teachings to writing. I suppose this practice began
originally for two reasons: they did not want their doctrines
to be accessible to the ordinary people, and they did not want
their pupils to rely on the written word and so neglect to train
their memories.*

JULIUS CAESAR, *DE BELLO GALLICO* 6.14

In order for myths to be created, there need to be individuals to
mould stories, to transmit them and to curate them. Celtic myths
present particularly complex intricacies because they were undoubtedly born long before literacy. For the greater part of the Iron Age
in Wales and Ireland, between around 700 BC and the 1st century
AD in Wales, or the 6th century AD in Ireland, a literary tradition
was absent. This means that although mythic stories must have cir-
culated in non-literate contexts when they were first constructed,
compilation of these narratives in writing came at a much later
stage of their existence.

• SPEAKING AND WRITING •

There is something about committing mythic – or any other –
stories to physical form that changes them, because such an act
codifies them, freeze-frames them and renders them less organic.
Writing is only one form of tangible recording. Another is image-
making, whether in the form of sculpture or painting. Many

cultures with a strong oral tradition, the San of southern Africa and the Aboriginal peoples of Australia to name just two, chose and still choose to commit their myths to rock-art. Change still occurs, for it is possible to paint over previous art and to add to picture-panels. In European antiquity, complex rock-carvings, in such areas as Galícia, North Italy and Scandinavia, undoubtedly record cosmological knowledge and sacred tales, although the key to understanding them eludes modern scholars. It is worth observing, though, that almost all sacred rock-art, whether it belonged to the ancient world or to more modern traditional societies, contains some common themes, notably the presence of shape-shifters, appearing in half-human, half-animal form. Of course, there can be no kind of direct cultural link across such vast zones of time and space, but what may be indicated is that the puzzle of being human predisposes people to represent things beyond their material world and, perhaps, to see animals as a gateway to accessing the spirit world. Shape-shifters are common protagonists in Celtic myths.

The Mabinogion tales of medieval Wales present an intricate tangle of oral and written narrative. Indeed, it is difficult to discern where one ends and the other begins. This is because, even in their written form, the tales were designed to be performed, not simply to be read. But even so, certain devices, the most obvious of which are the use of direct speech and repetition, betray oral origins. Another striking custom in the Welsh stories is the way that tenses change, in order to enhance dramatic effect. So, for instance, in the tale of 'Peredur', an historic narrative in the past tense, describing the context in which Peredur travelled to Arthur's court, is succeeded by an abrupt switch to the present tense, in order to highlight the drama and immediacy of the hero's arrival. This is done to make the audience sit up and take notice, and the storyteller probably changed his speaking tone to match the increased tension of the moment. (The context for the quotation overleaf is the insult done to Arthur's queen Gwenhwyfar by a nameless knight.)

*And they assumed that no one would commit such a crime
as that unless he possessed strength and power or magic and
enchantment so that no one could wreak vengeance on him.
With that Peredur comes into the hall on a bony, dapple-
grey nag....*

FROM 'PEREDUR'

● THE DRUIDS AND ORAL TRADITION ●

*For it usually does happen that if people have the help
of written documents, they do not pay as much attention
to learning by heart, and so let their memories become
less efficient.*

CAESAR, *DE BELLO GALLICO* 6.14

Words are powerful things, the more so if they are spoken aloud,
so that sound and meaning blend into a single powerful message
that can be shared simultaneously by many people. Keepers of oral
tradition had to have prodigiously long and accurate memories
and the ability to learn long tales by heart, while adding embellish-
ments along the way. Listeners, too, would remember stories they
had heard all their lives, and would not have hesitated to point out
errors or inconsistencies.

In his war-commentaries, Julius Caesar, writing of the Celts of
Gaul in the 50s BC, makes telling remarks about the Druidic priest-
hood and their responsibilities in the curation and dissemination of
oral doctrine. According to him, Druids were *the* religious authori-
ties in Gaul and Britain, and they frowned upon the committal of
traditions to writing. Although they were able to write (and, indeed,
they kept their accounts using the Greek alphabet), they considered
oral teaching better on two counts: first, a perceived need for the
confinement of knowledge to their chosen pupils, and secondly in
order to hone their students' skills in committing to memory what

Late Iron Age bronze figurine of a man holding an egg-like object, perhaps a Druid's egg, an object used in prophecy, from Neuvy-en-Sullias, in France.

they learned. The complexity of Welsh and Irish mythic texts testifies to the power of orally stored language. While the tales themselves undoubtedly changed over time (and this is what kept them alive and relevant to their listeners), it was vital that the names of people and places were passed down the generations, and that the kernel of mythic messages was not lost because of lapses in detailed memory.

Why was oral tradition so crucial to Celtic and other ancient societies? One reason is that it served to give individuals and communities a sense of rootedness. It explained natural phenomena, features in the landscape, past conflicts and disasters, putting them into a framework that people could relate to and comprehend. Word of mouth was very immediate and, above all, it was accessible to the majority, who were unable to read. In medieval Wales and Ireland, learning and writing were the preserve of the royal and noble courts, on the one hand, and the clergy, on the other. Heard myths and stories bound communities together, gave them a common heritage and a shared identity.

Book 6 of Caesar's military commentaries contains an ethnographic section in which he describes the Druids as religious leaders with wide-ranging powers. Significantly, the Roman general commented on their abilities as teachers, but the importance of the Druids lay in their far-reaching abilities to communicate with the world of the gods and the ancestral spirits. Caesar and other contemporary authors stressed their skill at all manner of prophecy, particularly divination (a method of tapping into the spirit-world and determining the wishes of the gods).

The close association between the Druids and the spirit-world is akin to the powers of modern shamans, among such traditions as those of the Siberian Sámi and Amazonian communities. This

Diviciacus the Druid

The system of divination is not even neglected among barbaric peoples, since in fact there are Druids in Gaul; I myself knew one of them, Diviciacus of the Aedui, who declared that he was acquainted with the system of nature which the Greeks call natural philosophy and he used to predict the future by both augury and inference.

CICERO, *DE DIVINATIONE* I, 90

Caesar wrote about his friend and ally, Diviciacus, who was the leader of the Burgundian tribe of the Aedui. But Caesar's near contemporary Cicero met the Gaulish chieftain when the latter visited Rome in 60 BC to ask for aid against his enemy, the German Ariovistus. Cicero was an urbane and accomplished Roman orator and man of letters, yet he admitted how impressed he was by Diviciacus's skill in divination: predicting the future and the will of the gods by ritual means. Diviciacus was pro-Roman, Caesar's friend. But he had a brother, Dumnorix, who loathed Rome and whose overriding desire was to oust the conquerors from Gallic territory. Because he did not trust him not to foment rebellion in his absence, Caesar 'invited' Dumnorix to accompany him on his British expedition. Dumnorix demurred, using his religious duties connectivity with the divine, coupled with their acknowledged powers as orators and keepers of oral tradition, makes these ancient Iron Age gurus ideal candidates for the job of myth-making.

• THE TRIPLEFOLD BARDIC MODEL •

The Sicilian Greek writers Diodorus Siculus and Strabo wrote during the time of both Julius Caesar and his heir, Augustus. Diodorus's *World History* (called the Βιβλιοθήκη), which comprised 40 books, contained detailed descriptions of the Gauls, though his information probably derived largely from earlier writers. Much of Strabo's

Scene showing the Gallic tribal leader and divinatory Diviciacus at Rome.

as an excuse. So both Aeduan brothers possessed sacred authority. Each may have been a Druid, but they were driven by very different allegiances.

Geography was likewise copied from earlier sources. Both of them wrote of three learned classes in Gaul: the lyric poets, called bards, whose role it was to sing praise poetry and satirical verse, while accompanying themselves on the lyre; the seers (*vates*), who had the responsibility for predicting the future by interpreting omens and portents, by means of human sacrifice; and the Druids, philosophers and theologians. So, while Caesar conflated all these sacred duties and skills under the umbrella of Druids, the Greek historians divided them into three distinct categories.

Both Caesar and Diodorus agree that present in Gaul (and Britain, according to Caesar) were a high class of individuals responsible for religious ritual, communication with the divine world and the curation of oral tradition. All three roles contribute to the creation of myths, including those associated with the ancestors. Dissemination of oral narratives about the past served to underpin and explain the existence of natural phenomena, such as rivers and mountains. Additionally, the monuments of pre-Iron Age communities, such as funerary mounds and standing stones, became woven into the tapestry of myth, and thus provided a cultural context for the Iron Age present.

Virtually the same triple-fold learned cast described by ancient Greek authors as being present in Gaul is attested in early Irish mythic tradition. Religion, divination, teaching and poetry were in the hands of the Druids, the *filidh* and the bards. By the 7th century AD, most of the pagan functions that remained after the adoption of Christianity were in the hands of the *filidh*. Whilst the Druids bore the brunt of Christian antagonism, and the bards' influence waned (partly because the *filidh* were stronger), the roles of the *filidh* as teachers, kingly advisers, poets, satirists (the political lampoonists of their day) and keepers of tradition were maintained for much longer. Indeed, it was not until the 17th century, under the relentless onslaught of the English government against the old Irish order, that the *filidh* disappeared.

Cathbad the Ulster Druid

The boy Conchobar was reared by Cathbad the Druid
and was known as Cathbad's son.
Fair-faced Cathbad – prince, pure, precious crown, grown huge in Druid spells.
FROM THE *TÁIN BÓ CUAILNGE*

Like their forebears in Iron Age Gaul and Britain, the Druids of Irish myth were principally concerned with divination, ascertaining the wishes of the gods. One such was Cathbad, who acted as adviser to the Ulster king Conchobar, and who repeatedly foretold the good or evil that would befall the Ulstermen. In one episode, narrated in a 9th-century text, Cathbad predicted that the unborn daughter of King Conchobar's court storyteller, Fedlimid, would be Deirdre, a beautiful girl but one who would cause slaughter and downfall for the men of Ulster by triggering internal conflict.

Cathbad taught the craft of divination to the young hero Cú Chulainn and his fellow Ulster champions. This involved instructing them on the interpretation of omens from the gods and on the auspicious and inauspicious days for events such as going to battle, inaugurating new kings and marriage. Most famously, Cathbad prophesied that anyone taking up arms on a particular day would have a glorious military career but would die young. The young man who did so was Cú Chulainn. His life and early death were exactly as Cathbad had predicted.

Deirdre of the Sorrows, grieving for her lover Naoise,
from a painting by John Duncan, 1900.

45

• GODS, PEOPLE AND BEASTS •

The early myth-spinners – whether they were Druids, bards or other storytellers – relied on their ability to tap into the world of the spirits. Celtic myths, like those of the Classical world, are laced with references to the close and symbiotic relationship between people and the gods. The spirit world was everywhere and the stories contain constant references to the presence of gods who participated in (and interfered with) humans and their activities. Cú Chulainn was beset by female deities, many of whom wished to make love to him. At his death, tied to a post so that he would not appear to bow before an enemy, the Badbh, in her role as goddess of the battlefield, perched on his shoulder in the form of a raven.

In 'modern' shamanism, animals play a pivotal role in mediating between the material and spirit worlds. They are often perceived as spirit-helpers, with the ability to cross the boundary between the realms of people and the spirits. This is also true of the Celtic mythic tradition, where animals – often birds or other wild creatures – take centre-stage in connecting gods and humans. The beginning of the First Branch of the *Mabinogi* illustrates such links very clearly, using the theme of the divine hunt (incidentally this recurs elsewhere in the Welsh storytellers' repertoire and in the cognate Irish texts). The hunt was a device for the myth-spinner to present direct contact between earth- and spirit-worlds: the hunter was mortal, but his quarry was sent from the Otherworld.

In this Welsh episode, the hunter was Pwyll, Lord of Llys Arberth, in southwest Wales. He was out in the forest with his hounds, and a stag had been scented. As Pwyll and his dogs sighted the deer, he saw another pack of dogs already engaged in bringing it down; this second pack was strange: dazzling white with red ears. In describing their colouring, the storyteller was tapping into another common Celtic mythical theme, for it was creatures from the spirit-world that had red or red-and-white coats. Pwyll urged on his own hounds

Iron Age rock-carving from Val Camonica, North Italy, depicting a half-human, half-stag creature.

and they routed the other pack but, as they did so, a horseman on a dapple-grey mount emerged from the forest and challenged Pwyll, railing at him for his discourtesy in stealing another's kill. Pwyll was contrite and asked what he could do to make amends, to which the strange horseman replied by introducing himself as Arawn, lord of his Otherworld kingdom Annwfn. Pwyll's retribution was to change places with Arawn for a year and a day and to fight and overcome another spirit-king Hafgan. In a sense, what the story-teller was doing was to make the audience anticipate an important event in the narrative. By hearing of a hunt, listeners would immediately realise that something peculiar and otherworldly was about to happen. The animals – the stag and the hounds – were the catalysts for the encounter.

Gildas

I shall not enumerate the devilish monstrosities of my land, numerous almost as those that plagued Egypt, some of which we can see today, stark as ever, inside or outside deserted city walls: outlines still ugly, faces still grim. I shall not name the mountains and hills and rivers, once so pernicious, now useful for human needs, on which, in those days, a blind people heaped divine honours.

FROM *LIVES OF THE SAINTS*

Gildas was a British monk who spent a lot of his time denouncing the pagan practices he observed in Britain during the 6th century AD (when the land had been officially Christian since the time of the Emperor Constantine in the early 4th century). Gildas is famous for having written a 'complaining book' (a *liber querulus*) entitled *De Excidio Britanniae*, in which he soundly condemned the lapsed morality of contemporary British rulers. The earliest surviving manuscript of this clerical diatribe dates to the 11th century but the *De Excidio* is thought to be a genuinely early work, probably written between AD 515 and 530. In it Gildas specifically mentions pagan monuments and traditions of worship that were anathema to him.

Gildas was not alone in his observations. His contemporary, the French 6th-century mystic Gregory of Tours, wrote a book entitled *The Glory of the Confessors*, in which he commented on a fellow cleric, Hilary, Bishop of Poitiers, who condemned pagan sacrificial practices that he alleged to have witnessed at a lake in the Cevennes.

● THE COMMITTAL OF EARLY MYTH TO WRITING ●

But how did the myths make the transition from word of mouth to paper? Given that education in medieval Ireland and Wales was restricted to the royal courts and the monasteries, it should be no surprise that Celtic myths have come down to us through the industry of Christian clerics or those educated by them. We know the myths pre-date the time they were written down because of the oral devices discussed above and in Chapter 1. Furthermore, they, especially the Irish mythologies, have a strong pagan pulse that is clear despite the fact that there is a fair amount of invention and anti-pagan propaganda written down by the Christian clerics; and there are striking similarities between the material culture of symbolism in later prehistory and recurrent themes in the written myths.

This evidence is archaeological, principally that of iconography and inscriptions, mostly belonging to the western Roman provinces of *Gallia* and *Britannia*, including Wales but excluding Ireland. Despite the inevitable Roman influence upon this assemblage of data, a great deal of native Gallic and British cosmology is discernible. It is likely that the influence of this early material on the later Celtic myths came about in two ways. First, it was conveyed through oral tradition, which probably began deep in prehistoric contexts. Secondly, we know from the comments of early Christian clerics, such as Gildas in the 6th century AD and, later, Giraldus Cambrensis (Gerald of Wales) in the 12th century, that some pagan monuments dating back at least to the Roman period survived visibly in the landscape.

The *peregrinatio pro Dei amore*

> *I am consumed with a desire so ardent that it casts every other thought and desire out of my heart. I have resolved, if it be God's will, to seek out the land of Promise of the Saints.*
> FROM THE *VOYAGE OF ST BRENDAN*

Early monks from Ireland and Wales travelled widely in Europe, answering to a perceived need to undertake a Christian *peregrinatio pro Dei amore* (a 'journey for the love of God'), a kind of spiritual quest whose purpose was to spread the Christian message, establish new monasteries and to find enlightenment by becoming close to God. One such monk was an Irish Christian called Columbanus, born in AD 543. He embraced the *peregrinatio* with tremendous zeal and fulfilled his search for God's presence by travelling widely in

Continental Europe, particularly in France. Pope Pius XI credited Columbanus with contributing more than any of his contemporaries to the Christian mission not only in France but also in Germany and Italy. Columbanus' journey began in northwest Ireland, at Abbot Sinell's monastery of Lough Erne (the location of the G8 Summit Conference on the Syrian Conflict).

Columbanus's story demonstrates the *peregrinatio* in action. This kind of clerical missionary travel (somewhat similar to the journeys undertaken by Saint Paul, as narrated in the Acts of the Apostles) most probably exposed early Christian monks to the sight of pagan religious sculptures and inscribed monuments. Some of the statues, temples and ritual objects they encountered might well have fuelled aspects of oral storytelling and may have found their way into the mythic tradition. It is difficult, otherwise, to explain the striking similarities between the religious archaeology of Iron Age and Roman Britain and Europe and elements present in the mythic narratives. The journeys of early clerics, such as Columbanus, may have created so-called 'corridors of time': conduits for the transference of tradition between later prehistory and the early medieval period.

Grounding Celtic Myths in a Cosmic Past

Caerleon is of unquestioned antiquity. It was constructed with great care by the Romans, the walls being built of brick. You can still see many vestiges of its one-time splendour.
GIRALDUS CAMBRENSIS, *THE JOURNEY THROUGH WALES*

To argue for the presence of true links between the archaeological evidence for pre-Christian religion in Britain and Gaul, on the one hand, and the medieval Celtic myths of Ireland and Wales, on the other, is a hazardous undertaking. However, the strange and complex mythic landscape of the Celtic West did not spring fully formed and without context into the early medieval consciousness.

Saint Brendan and a siren, from the German translation
of *Navigatio Sancti Brendani Abbatis*, c. 1476.

Rather, it was grounded in earlier cosmologies, as presented by archaeological testimony. To give an example, the Roman amphi-theatre at Caerleon was identified by medieval myth-makers as King Arthur's Round Table. The conduits for connections may well have been the storytellers, who saw relics from the past or who obtained information from others who reported seeing ancient remains on their travels. It is the job of storytellers to weave narratives around kernels of reality. It is satisfying to imagine that this was one way in which fragments of early beliefs and cult-practices have been preserved in the earliest mythic stories of the Celtic West, whatever transformations they may have undergone along the way.

Roman-period altar (from Germany) to Taranucnus, or Taranis, the Celtic thunder-god.

Archaeological evidence from the Roman period in Gaul and Britain presents a dazzling and dynamic array of Celtic gods and goddesses. Some, like Taranis, the thunder-god, Epona the horse-goddess, and the triple mother-goddesses spanned wide areas of Europe. Others, like the water-goddesses Sulis at Bath in the British West Country, Coventina at Carrawburgh on Hadrian's Wall and Sequana in Burgundy, were tied to one place and were the personifications of particular sacred springs or rivers. Taranis was a god of storms, but he was also a solar deity. His emblems were the sun-wheel, the eagle, the oak and the lightning-flash, and much of his imagery may have fed into the Welsh and Irish celestial myths, including those of the Welsh hero Lleu (see pp. 135–37) and Irish Lugh (see pp. 67–68). Tales of the battles that Lugh fought with the monsters of evil, the Fomorians, may well contain remnants of Taranis's battle with the Otherworld giant, with its half-human, half-serpentine body. In the same way, the ancient goddesses of springs may provide the foundation of Irish myths such as that of Boann, goddess of the great river Boyne. The Welsh heroine Rhiannon is surely closely linked with the ancient Gallic horse-goddess Epona. The triple mother-goddesses, such popular objects of veneration in Roman Britain and Europe, were surely the inspiration for the fearsome Irish triads, the Morrigna and the Badbh.

• MYTHS, MONKS AND MANUSCRIPTS •

The fact that the people who wrote down the myths were monks presents a conundrum. Were it not for the action of early Christian scribes, the myths would have been entirely lost. On the other hand, what were the monks doing when they committed pagan myths to manuscript? It is always possible that they saw it as their duty to preserve the oral heritage of the Celtic world. But it is more likely that they used the stories of old gods and supernatural beings, such

An Ancient Goddess in a Medieval Myth: Epona and Rhiannon

And Pwyll thought that at the second leap or the third he would catch up with her. But he was no closer to her than before. He urged his horse to go as fast as possible. But he saw that it was useless for him to pursue her.

FROM THE FIRST BRANCH OF THE *MABINOGI*

The First Branch of the *Mabinogi* contains a description of a magical woman, Rhiannon, who appeared to Pwyll, Lord of Llys Arberth, as a horsewoman, while he was sitting on the *Gorsedd Arberth*, an enchanted hill. The *Gorsedd* was a place that caused supernatural events to occur to those who sat there: either something wonderful or catastrophic. Neither he nor his fleetest horsemen could catch up with her despite the slow place of her mount, but when in desperation he called out to her she immediately reined in her horse. Introducing herself as Rhiannon, she said that she had been waiting for him to speak to her. After a time of courtship, they were married and had a son, Pryderi, to whom his mother bequeathed her horse-affinities (see pp. 112–15).

The name Rhiannon derives from a Roman-period British goddess called Rigantona, 'Sacred Queen'. This alone gives her a supernatural

as the Daghdha, Medbh, the Morrigán, Rhiannon and Manawydan (the protagonists of following chapters), in order to denigrate and ridicule paganism and to twist the tales so that they encapsulated Christian codes of conduct and ethics. In the Ulster Cycle and the Mabinogion, for instance, war is presented as pointlessly destructive. In most of the Irish texts, powerful women are not treated with any great sympathy and over-enthusiastic sexual behaviour is frowned upon. If the mythic texts were written not by clergy but their pupils, this allows for some flexibility and some imaginative writing not so hidebound by Christian ethics.

Before following through on the connection between the myths and Christian literary tradition, the link between oral stories and

dimension. But the circumstances of her first encounter with Pwyll betray her spiritual origins: white was the colour of Otherworld animals, and her ability to outpace Pwyll's swiftest steeds while she was riding quite slowly, once again displays her supernatural genesis. It is possible that the origins of the Rhiannon myth lay in an important early goddess, worshipped in the Roman period in Gaul, Britain and widely spread over much of Europe. Her name was Epona ('Horse-Goddess') and she was depicted in imagery riding side-saddle on a mare or sitting between two horses. Monuments to Epona may still have been visible to wandering monks in the early medieval period, and may have been the inspiration for the story of Rhiannon.

Bronze figurine of the horse-goddess Epona, seated between two ponies, with ears of corn; from an unprovenanced site in Wiltshire.

written tales needs to be considered. Over long periods of time, successions of storytellers would have tweaked, adapted and added to core tales, to suit the times and the environment in which the bards were working. So, perhaps, when performing as entertainers at royal courts, aspects of courtly love and knightly rivalry might be in the forefront of the repertoire. More intimate storytelling, around the domestic fire at night, might have inspired more imaginative tales, of weird monsters and wayward spirits.

It would be a mistake to assume that the mythic literature of medieval Ireland and Wales came into being simply as the result of copying down orally transmitted tales. Although the kernel of this literature drew heavily upon heard tales, the texts show all the

Iolo Morgannwg and the Modern Welsh Bardic Tradition

Iolo, old Iolo, he who knows
the virtues of all herbs of mount and vale....
Whatever lore of science or of song
sages and bards of old have handed down.

FROM AN EARLY 19TH-CENTURY POEM BY ROBERT SOUTHEY

Every summer in Wales, a huge cultural festival takes place at a
different location alternately in North and South Wales. This is the
Welsh National Eisteddfod, and at its core is the Assembly of Bards
(the *Gorsedd y Beirdd*). The central foci of the Eisteddfod are the Welsh
language prose and poetry competitions, culminating in three events:
the Crowning of the Bard, the Chairing of the Bard and the award of the
Prose Medal. The festival is not new but neither is it very old. The current
tradition was the invention of an 18th-century Glamorgan stonemason
called Edward Williams, who renamed himself Iolo Morgannwg.
He, and like-minded men, deeply worried about the decline of the
Welsh language, sought to revivify it and Welsh tradition in general by
'constructing' a pedigree and an ancestry for Wales that led back to the
ancient Druids. While the Welsh bardic tradition can be traced back
at least until the 12th century, it was Iolo who added to it a backdrop
of elaborate theatre, beginning with the establishment of the *Gorsedd
Beirdd Ynys Prydain* (the Assembly of the Bard of Britain) on Primrose
Hill in London in 1792. Iolo's legacy is the annual Eisteddfod, and it is
perhaps permissible to identify today's bardic competitors, who seek to
express Welsh tradition through strictly regulated poetry and prose, as
modern 'myth-spinners'.

signs of deliberate literary construction. Stories were codified and
organized to suit the work of scribes. The old tales were laced with
contemporary material that brought them up to date and provided
present-day readers with subtle insights into life in the medieval
Celtic West.

Attempts to assign individual authorship of the Welsh and Irish mythological texts have been largely unsuccessful. Some scholars have argued with conviction that the Four Branches of the *Mabinogi* were the work of either Sulien, Bishop of Saint David's in the far west of Pembrokeshire, or of his son Rhigyfarch, but there is no hard evidence for such ascription. Unlike the early Insular medieval mythic tales, the pagan element in the Welsh literature is sometimes half-buried under a layer of overt Christianity: for instance, when the enchanted boar Twrch Trwyf was asked how he came to be cursed with an animal shape, he replied that God had transformed him and his followers because of his wickedness. So, despite probable origins in pre-Christian oral tales, medieval Welsh scribes appear to have indicated pagan roots not by describing gods and goddesses but in more subtle ways, in their references to talking heads, shape-shifting, Otherworld beings and magical places.

The Irish myths are different. They are bursting with pagan deities, prophets, Druids and semi-divine heroes; kings and queens interact freely with the supernatural world. The overt pagan flavour of Irish mythology convinces many scholars of its genuinely ancient origins. But others argue with equal certainty that medieval Irish clerics worked staunchly within a Christian context, using both the Classical and Biblical texts available to them, to construct a spurious archaism that allowed them to present Christian messages and codes of ethics by exaggerating the immoderate, bellicose and promiscuous antics of pagans.

The Welsh and Irish stories are very different from each other both in content and in timbre. But there are also marked similarities as we have seen in Chapter 1: speaking heads, transformation between human and animal-form, magical cauldrons and the presence of an earth-like Otherworld. It is highly likely that storytellers travelled freely between the courts of Ireland and Wales, and the sharing of storylines between the two countries is not hard to explain.

3

A PLETHORA OF IRISH SPIRITS

Now it was that the Morrigan settled in bird shape on a
standing stone in Temair Cuailnge, and said to the Brown Bull:
'Dark one are you restless.
Do you guess they gather
to certain slaughter
the wise raven
groans aloud
that enemies infest
the fair fields.'
FROM THE *TÁIN BÓ CUAILNGE*

The medieval mythic texts of Ireland differ sharply from those of Wales in their overt paganism and in the presence of a constellation of divine beings. Whilst the Welsh myths contain repeated references to the Christian God, the cognate Irish texts do not. The Irish legends are steeped in the activities of deities whose behaviour would not have been out of place in the Classical pantheons. Gods of fertility, water, battle, the sun, blacksmithing, craft-working and the Otherworld played out their dramas in the theatre of storytelling. The three principal 'cycles' of Irish tales are the *Táin Bó Cuailnge* (The Cattle Raid of Cooley), the Mythological Cycle, with its two main books – the *Leabhar Gabhála* (The Book of Invasions) and the *Dinnshenchas* (The History of Places) – and the Fenian (or Fionn) Cycle. Other major sources include the 11th-century Yellow Book of Lecan, which contains the account of 'Da Derga's Hostel', a chilling tale of the Irish Otherworld and its dreadful goddess of death.

• CREATION TALES •

The first invaders of Ireland were fifty-one women and three men. They were descended from Noah himself and all except a single man died in the Flood. Fintan was the sole survivor, and he had the gift of magic. So he changed himself into a salmon so that he could swim through the flood water. As the water level dropped, he changed again, into an eagle and then a hawk, so that he could fly high above the emerging land and could see the mountains and plains reappearing as the water subsided.

FROM THE BOOK OF INVASIONS

It is a function of myth to produce explanations of people's origins. A 12th-century text known as the Book of Invasions provides just such a context for the presence of the Gaels (or Celts) in Ireland. As its name suggests, it chronicles waves of 'invasions', beginning with an expedition led by a woman called Cesair, of whom virtually nothing is known except that she is said to be the granddaughter of Noah. The book contains a reference to the Great Flood, immediately after which a man called Partholón led another wave of colonists. He fought a fierce battle with the Fomorians (Irish *Fomhoire*), a race of monsters already inhabiting Ireland.

The central theme of the Book of Invasions, however, is the colonization of Ireland by a race of gods known as the Tuatha Dé Danann (the People of the Goddess Danu). They ruled the land until driven out in their turn by the Gaels, whose presence forced the Tuatha Dé Danann to retreat underground and create an Otherworld realm parallel to the earthly world. These dispossessed gods lived in *sídhe*, spirit mounds (perhaps like that at Newgrange – see figure overleaf), each of which had a hostel or *bruidhen*, in which they hosted perpetual feasts.

Aerial view of the great Neolithic passage-grave at Newgrange, Ireland. In early Irish mythology, ancient tombs like these were thought to be the abodes of the spirits.

• THE IRISH PANTHEON •

A couple of thousand years ago there lived in Ireland a people who were gods and the children of gods. They were of radiant beauty and godlike bearing, and they loved above all things poetry, music and beauty of form in man and woman. These beautiful people were descended from the goddess Dana, and so were called the Dan Danaans, or the people of Dana.

FROM THE BOOK OF INVASIONS

Despite the wide range of divinities present in the mythic stories, there was no clear sky-father-god, like Zeus or Jupiter in the Classical pantheons, although Lugh, as a god of light, comes closest to a celestial deity, and the Daghdha was lord of all the gods. There

The Talismans of the Tuatha Dé Danann

Whence the Tuatha Dé Danann came is not recorded in the written myths, but they traced their ancestry to a founder-goddess Danu. When they arrived in Ireland, they brought four precious, magical and powerful objects with them. One, the Stone of Fál, (see pp. 171–72) was linked to Sacral Kingship: when a new ruler was being vetted for election, the Stone would shriek if touched by the rightful claimant. The other three were all connected with individual gods and served to empower them. The Cauldron of Regeneration belonged to the Daghdha, the Good God, and was never empty of food; the Spear of Lugh ensured that this warrior-god would always prevail over his enemies; and the Sword of Nuadu was wielded by this weather-god and from its stroke none could survive.

was no single war-god, like Ares and Mars, but a number of war-deities, most of them female. There was no overt goddess of erotic love on the model of Aphrodite/Venus, but many goddesses – such as the Morrigán and the queen-goddess Medbh – had their promiscuous side.

There were powerful fertility gods, including the Daghdha; goddesses associated with sovereignty and prosperity, such as Ériu; and a cluster of functional deities, such as Dian Cécht (who combined the roles of Healer and Craftsman) and Goibhniu the Smith, whose weapons never missed their mark. This last god, like many of the others, had an Otherworld hostel: those who partook of his feasts acquired immortality. There is no doubt that the redaction of Irish myths by Christian clerics had a huge influence on the way the Irish pantheon was presented. War-deities were evil women with unbridled sexual appetites, and even the Daghdha was portrayed as a ridiculously bloated and bibulous figure.

The Principal Irish Gods of the Tuatha Dé Danann

The Daghdha	Chief of the gods; divine guarantor of fertility and prosperity
Lugh	God of war, light and craft skills
Macha	A horse and battle goddess
The Morrigán	Goddess of war and death
The Badbh	Interchangeable with the Morrigán
Goibhniu	A smith-god
Dian Cécht	God of healing and crafts
Danu/Anu	Foundation goddesses
Ériu	Eponymous goddess of Ireland
Oenghus	God of lovers
Nuadu	The name means 'cloud-maker', so he may be a weather-god
Boann	Goddess of the river Boyne
Manannán	God of the sea

• A DIVINE TRIAD: DAGHDHA, BOANN AND OENGHUS •

There was over Ériu a famous king from the Tuatha Dé Danann and Echu Ollathir was his name. Another name for him was the Daghdha, for it was he who performed miracles and saw to the weather and the harvest, and that is why he was called the Good God.

FROM THE BOOK OF INVASIONS

The Daghdha was the tribal father-god, a principal deity of the pantheon. His title the 'Good God' indicates his primary role as guardian of Ireland's prosperity. Not only did he possess his magical cauldron of plenty but he also wielded a huge club, one end of which dealt death and the other restored life. The Daghdha was huge in all senses: his body was enormous and his belly immense; his sexual

Romano-British carving of Hercules wielding a club, a similar image to descriptions of the Irish Daghdha, from Corbridge, Northumberland.

appetite was prodigious, and he had intercourse with many divine women, including the Morrigán (seemingly his antithesis, in her destructive powers) and Boann, the river-goddess.

His union with the latter took place while she was still married to the water-god Nechtan. When she became pregnant by her lover, the couple sought to conceal their illicit partnership and the Daghdha did this by casting a spell on the sun so that it stood motionless in the heavens for nine months, neither rising nor setting. So the baby was effectively conceived and born on the same day. The child was a boy, and they named him Oenghus mac Oc, 'Son of the Young' or 'The Youth', in recognition of the weird solar event surrounding his birth. Oenghus became a god of love, a champion of young star-crossed couples.

Stone carving of the sky-god Jupiter trampling a giant, on a column from Neschers, France.

• NUADU OF THE SILVER ARM •

Nuadu Argatlámh ('Silver Arm') was once the king of the Tuatha Dé Danann. But there was a strict rule in Irish mythic lore that a king had to be physically perfect, with no blemishes or abnormalities. Nuadu's arm was hacked off in battle and so, no longer whole, he had to abdicate. But another god, Dian Cécht, came to his aid. He was a divine physician, skilled in the craft of healing, but he also had power as a metal smith. He made Nuadu a new arm and hand out of silver, perhaps the first prosthetic limb recorded in early mythology.

Thus restored to his full form, Nuadu was able to re-assume his kingship. However, he had become exhausted by constant fighting with the Fomorians, monsters who were sworn enemies of the Tuatha Dé Danann and soon after his new limb had been fitted, he relinquished the leadership of the gods to another much younger god, Lugh. The name Nuadu may mean 'cloud-maker', hinting at his original function as a god of weather and storms, like the Classical Zeus/Jupiter.

Nuadu and Nodens

It is not often possible to make direct connections between the gods of medieval Celtic myth and the early native divinities worshipped in Roman Britain. But a promising candidate for such association is the British god Nodens, whose principal sanctuary was at Lydney in the Forest of Dean, overlooking the broad river Severn close to its estuary. Nodens's name is cognate with that of Nuadu, and both may have been 'cloud-makers', lords of the sky and the weather. The temple at Lydney was built in the mid-4th century AD, when Christianity had already become established as the state religion of the Roman Empire. The shrine was excavated in the 1920s by Sir Mortimer Wheeler, who found inscriptions indicating that the shrine was dedicated to Nodens. The finds from the temple reveal that Nodens was a hunter–healer deity. Among the votive offerings were nine figurines of dogs, the most splendid being a model of a young deerhound (the great country house at Lydney still has a deer-park in its grounds).

A mosaic that once glorified the interior of the sanctuary bears an inscription telling of the presence there of an 'interpreter of dreams', presumably those experienced by sick pilgrims as they slept in the sacred dormitory hoping for a curative vision of the god. There was a bath-house here, and sick and injured devotees would bathe in the

Replica of the late Romano-British bronze deerhound from the temple of Nodens at Lydney.

The Curse and the Ring

One of the most telling objects from Lydney is a small lead tablet on which a curse was inscribed. These curses, known in the ancient world as *defixiones*, or 'fixing spells', were often dedicated at healing shrines. The goddess Sulis Minerva at Bath was addressed in numerous such curse-tablets placed in the sacred spring. The Lydney one is especially interesting because of the message it contains. The curse is dedicated to Nodens by a man called Silvianus. He had lost a gold ring at the temple, perhaps having taken it off with his clothes before bathing in the holy water. The curse indicates that Silvianus suspected that the thief was known to him, a fellow pilgrim named Senicianus, and it asks Nodens to blight the thief with ill-health until the ring is brought back to the temple. In return, Silvianus promises to give the god half of the ring's value.

This story is interesting enough, but there is more. A gold ring engraved with the name Senicianus has actually been found at the Roman city of Silchester in Hampshire. Could it be the same ring, audaciously inscribed with the name of the robber? The final dénouement of the Lydney curse is that one of the visitors to the site when Wheeler was digging it was none other than J. R. R. Tolkien. He was fascinated by Nodens, the curse and the ring, and shortly afterwards he began writing *The Hobbit*. Was he influenced by what he encountered on his visit to Lydney?

iron-rich spring-water in the hope that they would be healed by its touch. The temple at Lydney was situated deep in ancient woodland, high up with an uninterrupted view of the Severn and its dramatic tidal Bore that sweeps down it at certain high tides. If Nodens, like Nuadu, was a weather-god, his priests may well have claimed the power to predict the Bore as Nodens's divine action.

• LUGH OF THE LONG ARM: •
THE GOD OF LIGHT AND RIGHT

At the time when Nuadu felt his power failing, a young man, Lugh (whose name means 'Shining One'), appeared at the royal court of Tara and asked for admittance. The doorkeeper demanded to know what special skill the visitor possessed, since nobody without one was allowed to enter the court. Lugh replied that he was a carpenter, but the doorkeeper said they already had one; so he said he was a smith, then a harper, a hero, a praise poet, a sorcerer, a doctor, a cup-bearer and a craftsman. When the guardian of the gate told him that Tara already had one of each, Lugh retorted that his special gifts lay in his ability with all of these skills. He was permitted access to the court and to the king. Soon, he replaced Nuadu as king of the gods, using his multiple skills to lead his divine people.

• BATTLES WITH MONSTERS •

The Tuatha Dé Danann did not have Ireland handed to them on a plate when they invaded. They had to fight two separate groups of monstrous beings before they could establish themselves. The first were the Fir Bholg, who had taken over the land before the Tuatha Dé Danann arrived. It was at the First Battle of Magh Tuiredh in Co. Sligo that Nuadu lost his arm. Despite that setback, the race of gods was eventually victorious. Now they had to fight another enemy, the Fomorians.

Once Lugh had become king of the Tuatha Dé Danann, his principal task was to continue the battle against this second race of monsters. They were a formidable enemy. Lugh mustered all the wizardry and magical craft skills of his people in order to fashion invincible weapons and spells against their monstrous foe. Under Lugh's magic, the mountains were hurled upon them, and all

Ireland's water hidden from them. Druids were summoned to cast fire upon them and to make them ill.

The war between the Tuatha Dé Danann and the Fomorians culminated in the Second Battle of Magh Tuiredh, a bloody fight with many casualties on both sides. But the Tuatha Dé Danann had one huge advantage: while the slain Fomorians stayed dead, the gods were reborn by being cast into a magical well. The craft god Dian Cécht (he who had given Nuadu his new arm) and his three children sang spells over the well and the dead warriors were restored to life to join battle with the monsters once again. Lugh himself used magic to inspire his army. He moved among the soldiers chanting incantations to make them strong.

Balor of the Baleful Eye

The Fomorians had a fearsome champion named Balor. His single eye was so enormous that it took four men to raise the eyelid. When the eye was open, its gaze was so poisonous that, like Medusa's stare, it could freeze an entire army in its tracks; no one could survive it. When faced with this awful opponent, Lugh acted swiftly. As soon as Balor's eye swivelled in his direction, he took his sling and aimed straight for it. The force of the slingstone drove Balor's great eye right through his head so that it popped out at the back and turned its fatal gaze onto the Fomorians themselves. The Battle of Magh Tuiredh was over. The half-Fomorian king Bres, who had ruled Ireland briefly – and unsuccessfully – when Nuadu was disabled, was allowed to live in return for his advice to the Tuatha Dé Danann on farming practice.

Lugh's skill with the sling gave him his sobriquet Lugh Lámfhada ('Long Arm'). A divine figure with a virtually identical name is found in Welsh legend. This was Lleu Llaw Gyffes, the Bright One of the Skilful Hand. It is almost certain that these two Welsh and Irish gods shared a common identity, for each represented light and goodness, and skill at craftsmanship.

Oenghus mac Oc was the god of love, like Eros and Cupid in Classical mythology. His main job was to help star-crossed lovers, and the Book of Invasions contains many love-stories associated with him. But in one of the most romantic tales, 'The Dream of Oenghus', it is the god himself who was possessed by an 'impossible' love after he met a girl in a dream. Upon waking, he realized he was desperately in love with his dream-maiden and set out to discover who she was and how to find her.

The girl's name was Caer Ibormeith ('Yew-Berry'). Eventually, Oenghus tracked her down to a lake where she dwelt with a bevy of other young women. But Caer and her companions were not ordinary girls for, every other year at the Feast of Samhain (the cele-bration marking the end of the old Celtic year), when time stood still and the gateway between earth-world and the realm of the spirits stood open, they were transformed into swans. Caer herself was of supernatural origin; not only could she shape-shift, but her father was also clearly divine, for he had his own *sídh* (Otherworld palace). Each pair of girl–swans was linked together by a silver chain. But Caer herself was distinguished by being alone and having a chain of gold.

Caer's father refused Oenghus permission to wed his daugh-ter, but the young god persisted in his love. Realizing that he could only win her when she was in her swan-form, he went to the lake at Samhain-tide and called to her. When she came to him, he turned himself into a swan and took flight with her. The pair circled the lake three times, singing a spell as they went, so that everyone beneath them fell fast asleep and could not pursue them. Oenghus and Caer flew off to Oenghus's palace at Brugh na Bóinne and, perhaps, lived happily ever after.

The silver chains binding the swan-pairs have never been explained. Because the birds shape-shifted to the form of human maidens, it is always assumed that the swans were also female. But it is possible that the chained pairs of birds represented cobs and pens, the chain reflecting their monogamy and lifelong partnership. The fact that only Caer had a gold chain all to herself perhaps suggests her single state and her future marriage to a god.

● MIDHIR AND ÉTAIN ●

Midhir had decked himself out splendidly. He had brushed out his long golden hair and put on his slim golden headband. Wearing his purple tunic he stood heroically at the gate of the castle holding a spear of pointed bronze and a large circular shield ornamented with jewels. His shining grey eyes sparkled as he began the wooing of Étain.

FROM 'THE WOOING OF ÉTAIN' IN THE BOOK OF INVASIONS

Like Oenghus, Midhir was one of the Tuatha Dé Danann, lord of the *sídh* of Bri Léith. He fell deeply in love with a girl called Étain, who was mortal but in possession of some supernatural powers, such as the ability to hum Midhir to sleep and to warn him in advance that an enemy was drawing near. Midhir's wife Fuamnach was very jealous of his new love and, in her vengeful rage, cast a spell on the girl so that she was turned successively into a pool of water and a purple fly. Not content with this, Fuamnach conjured a wind that blew away the fly. But now Oenghus, divine champion of lovers, stepped in to rescue the hapless changed girl, and hid her at his palace on the Boyne. Fuamnach's curse was a strong one. Oenghus strove to overturn it but only partially succeeded, managing to restore Étain to human form at night-time.

Alas, Fuamnach's magic wind blew Étain away once again and the transformed fly dropped into a goblet of wine and was swallowed by Edar, the wife of an Ulster hero. This episode marked the end of Étain's first existence. She was reborn as a new baby a thousand years afterwards. But Midhir still searched for her and eventually tracked her down. Grown up, she had married Eochaidh, king of Ireland, who had wed her only because his people refused to comply with his tax-laws unless he had a wife. Midhir used his divine powers to win back Étain. He stole a kiss that triggered the memory of her first love. The two escaped from the king's court at Tara and, like Oenghus and Caer, the happy pair flew away as swans.

The tale of Midhir and Étain is steeped in divinity and magic: shape-changing, longevity and rebirth are all marks of the supernatural. The ability to effect transformation was facilitated by the timing: Samhain was a time of 'not being', when order disintegrated and chaos ruled.

Stone carving of Mercury (with a cockerel) and Rosmerta (with a bucket, ladle and sceptre) from Gloucester. They are cognate with the Irish divine couple Midhir and Étain.

The Symbolism of Swans

A feature of many Irish myths, including the love-stories of Oenghus and Caer, and Midhir and Étain, is transformation into swans. Swans are charismatic birds: large, white, beautiful and sometimes fierce, although often seen swimming serenely on the calm surface of the water. Waterfowl possessed powerful symbolism in Celtic myths because they are at home in all elements: water, air and land. The dazzling plumage of swans perhaps gave them an extra edge as it evoked purity; and their monogamous habit of pairing for life made them icons of faithful and enduring devotion, highly appropriate for divine lovers. Storytellers gave swans a much better press than their antitheses, the crow and the raven, black carrion birds that often foretold disaster and picked over the slain on the battlefield.

Early Iron Age bronze flesh-fork, used in feasting, from Dunaverney, Co. Antrim, Ireland.

• FATAL ATTRACTION: •
LOVE TRIANGLES IN IRISH MYTH

Cathbad placed his hand on the woman's stomach and prophesied that the unborn child would be a girl named Deirdre, and that she would be exceedingly beautiful but would bring about the ruin of Ulster.
FROM THE *TÁIN BÓ CUAILNGE*

A recurrent theme in stories about the Irish gods is that of the love triangle between an old husband (or fiancé), a young suitor and a young girl. This is probably a disguised myth of sovereignty wherein an old king is challenged by a young claimant to the throne. The young girl in the middle of the triangle may be identified with the goddess of sovereignty, whose power of granting prosperity to the land had to be won by means of sexual union with the young pretender. If the land needed revivifying, the old mortal king had to be deposed in favour of vigorous youth. The tale of Oenghus and Caer follows this theme to a degree, although in this case the older man was Caer's father, not a king. Indeed, there is a similar pattern in the Welsh mythic story of 'Culhwch and Olwen' (see pp. 129–30): Olwen's father – like Caer's – forbade her marriage to her young lover Culhwch.

Two Irish stories provide dramatic illustration of these jealous tensions between youth and old age. One is located within a 9th-century text that forms part of the Ulster Cycle, a precursor of the *Táin Bó Cuailnge*, which records the relationship between King Conchobar, his foster-daughter Deirdre and her lover Naoise. The second is found in a 10th-century tale, later incorporated into the 12th-century Fenian Cycle. It relates the love of Diarmaid and Gráinne, the betrothed wife of Finn, ageing leader of the war-band called the Fianna.

The life of Deirdre, often known as Deirdre of the Sorrows, was predicted by Cathbad the Ulster court Druid before she was born. Cathbad foretold that the child would grow up to be stunningly beautiful but that she would bring disaster to Ulster. Despite the Ulstermen's urgent appeal to Conchobar that the baby should be killed at birth, the king defied their advice and decided to rear her in secret as his foster-daughter. As the girl reached puberty, Conchobar noticed how lovely she was and desired her for his wife. Sequestered as she was, Deirdre had had little to do with men, but one day she caught sight of her foster-father as he had killed a calf and was skinning it, while a raven drank up the spilled blood. Snow lay upon the ground, and Deirdre was struck by the startling juxtaposition of the three colours: white, red and black. She vowed that the man she chose to marry would be raven-haired, white-skinned and red-cheeked.

Now Deirdre had a companion (perhaps more likely a chaperone) called Leabharcham; she let Deirdre know that there was indeed someone who fulfilled these criteria: his name was Naoise and he had two brothers. Unlike other love-triangle tales, in this instance it was Deirdre who made the running. She approached Naoise, but her reputation as a potential source of harm to Ulster had gone before her and he refused her overtures. Then Deirdre sought to win him over by a sure means: that of challenging his honour, threatening that he would be shamed if he did not elope with her.

The two ran away to Scotland with Naoise's brothers, but Conchobar summoned them back to Emhain Macha (see pp. 142–43), sending an envoy, Ferghus mac Roich, to pledge them a free pardon. The promise proved false. The vindictive king employed a man called Eoghan to kill Naoise and his two brothers. Deirdre's punishment was to be forcibly wed to her lover's murderer, but she took her own life rather than submit to him. Ferghus was angered by Conchobar's perfidy. There was bitter fighting between them that culminated in Ferghus and his followers splitting away from the Ulster court and defecting to Ulster's arch-enemy, Medbh of Connacht, thus fulfilling Cathbad's prophecy about the doom Deirdre would wreak upon her people.

The story of Finn, Diarmaid and Gráinne follows an essentially similar pattern to that of Conchobar, Deirdre and Naoise. Like Deirdre, it was Gráinne who was the instigator of the love affair with Diarmaid, even though she was engaged to Finn. Her betrayal of Finn suggests that, like her Ulster counterpart, Gráinne was a covert sovereignty goddess who spurned her elderly mortal consort and sought a youthful marriage partner in order to safeguard and reinvigorate Ireland's prosperity. Like Naoise, Diarmaid demurred when Gráinne made advances to him. He was in a difficult position for he was Finn's war-lieutenant and honour-bound to be loyal to his patron.

Neolithic tomb known as the 'Bed of Diarmaid', at Kilcooney, Co. Donegal, Ireland.

But, in exactly the same way as Deirdre, Gráinne struck at the roots of Diarmaid's honour as a hero. He was thus in a double-bind, with no escape. He submitted to Gráinne and the pair fled from Tara, where Finn presided. The elderly jilted suitor initiated a pursuit of the errant pair and this went on for seven years. But the ill-starred couple were not alone. Oenghus, the god of love, also happened to be Diarmaid's foster-father. He tried to help them, warning the pair never to sleep in the same place two nights running. The fugitives gained virtual immortality by eating the berries of the Tree of Immortality that grew in the enchanted forest of Duvnos. This meant that they could only be slain by means of a stronger spell than that of the tree's fruit.

Like Conchobar, Finn resorted to trickery. Apparently reconciled to his rival, he invited Diarmaid to join him on a boar-hunt. This was cunning, for Finn was aware of a prophecy that Diarmaid would be killed by a particular animal, the Boar of Boann Ghulban. This creature was a shape-shifter: he had once had human form and was none other than Diarmaid's foster-brother. Two versions of Diarmaid's death are recorded in the texts. According to one, the spines on the boar's back were tipped with poison, and the young man died when his skin was pierced by one of these bristles. The second one laid the blame on Finn himself. The old war-leader could have saved him by bringing him water. Three times he brought water from a sacred well in his cupped hands and twice he let it drain away as he reached the stricken youth. When he brought the life-giving water to Diarmaid the third time he meant to give it to him, but he was too late: Diarmaid was dead.

• THE GAELS AND THE GODDESSES •

The Gaels or Celts (sometimes known as the Milesians in the texts) were the final colonizers of Ireland, according to the Book of Invasions. They threw out the Tuatha Dé Danann, who took refuge underground in their Otherworld palaces (or *sídhe*). The Tuatha De Danann's origin-goddess Danu had three rivals, all more powerful than her. These goddesses each personified the land of Ireland and they met the new Gael invaders when they arrived. The trio were called Ériu, Fódla and Banbha. They were also rivals and each one demanded allegiance from the Gaels and a promise that they would name the land after her. In return, the victorious goddess pledged that the Gaels would keep Ireland for ever.

Ériu emerged as the winner and became the eponymous divine ancestress of Ireland (Érin is still used as an alternative name for the land today). Ériu was the original goddess of sovereignty and sacral kingship. Unlike many of Ireland's female deities, Ériu belonged to the whole of Ireland, and she was the essence of the land, its fertility and its success as a prosperous nation. Her supremacy at the time the Gaels invaded was foretold by the *filidh* Amhairghin, gifted not only to tell the future, but also to liaise with the spirits.

• 4 •

ENCHANTED WALES: A MAGICAL LAND

*Pwyll made for the top of a mound that was above the court,
called Gorsedd Arberth.*
*'Lord', said one of the court, 'the strange thing about the
mound is that whatever nobleman sits on it will not leave
there without one of two things happening: either he will be
wounded or injured, or else he will see something wonderful.'*
FROM THE FIRST FRANCH OF THE *MABINOGI*

The Welsh myths are mostly found in what we know as the
Mabinogion. Its Four Branches consist of four related but self-
contained stories. The First Branch tells the tale of Pwyll, lord of
Arberth, Arawn, god of Annwfn (the Otherworld), and Pwyll's wife
Rhiannon. The Second Branch is about Brân, lord of Harlech, his
sister Branwen and her husband Matholwch. The Third Branch tells
of the enchantment of Dyfed, and the adventures of Manawydan
and Pryderi, son of Pwyll. The Fourth Branch revolves around Math,
lord of Gwynedd, his nephews Gwydion and Gilfaethwy, and the
doom-laden marriage between Lleu Llaw Gyffes and Blodeuwedd.

As well as the Four Branches of the *Mabinogi*, there are several
other longer tales, namely the story of 'Culhwch and Olwen', a quest
in which the eponymous hero strives to win Olwen by accom-
plishing impossible deeds; 'The Spoils of Annwfn'; 'The Dream of
Rhonabwy'; and 'Peredur'. These all add to a sparkling tapestry of
spirits, demi-gods, enchanted creatures, magical cauldrons, magicians, shape-shifting and battles between good and evil.

Comparison between the Welsh and Irish mythic traditions
throws up major differences between them, notably in the extent
to which paganism is overtly displayed. Despite the monastic
genesis of the written Irish myths, they are brimming with gods and

goddesses and would appear to present a thoroughly pagan, poly-theistic (multi-deity) religious system. With the exception of the early *Lives* of Saints Brigit, Patrick and their peers, Christian Irish literature is more or less absent. But although paganism is clearly present in the Welsh mythic tradition, it is more muted. References are made to God, a prime example being the comment made by the enchanted boar Twrch Trwyth, in 'Culhwch and Olwen', that it was God who had changed him from human to animal form because of his evil ways. Heroes such as Brân the Blessed, Pwyll, Pryderi and Lleu Llaw Gyffes are presented as 'watered-down gods', as are noble-women, such as Rhiannon and Branwen.

The divine ancestor-figure Llyr produced many of the main pro-tagonists of the Welsh mythic stories: Brân the Blessed and Branwen, Gofannon and Manawydan. The last two have close Irish divine counterparts: Goibhniu the smith-god and the sea-god Manannán, the son of Lir (cognate with the Welsh Llyr). Close scrutiny of the Welsh tales reveals the presence of other pagan deities too. How else can we interpret Mabon the Hunter, helper of Culhwch in his quest? He must surely be identifiable with the archaeologically attested Gallo-British god Maponus, whose name was linked with that of the Classical hunter-god Apollo. The horse-symbolism of Rhiannon marks her out as of divine origin. She may well have developed from the Gallo-British horse-goddess Epona (see p. 54).

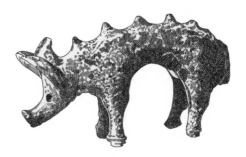

Bronze figurine of a boar from Hounslow, Middlesex (near London).

Owl face mount on the Iron Age cauldron from Brå, Denmark.

• THE WELSH PANTHEON AND HEROES •

If the Welsh gods appear pallid in comparison with the rich pantheon of Ireland, Welsh mythology makes up for it in its saturation with the supernatural. There are magicians and magical occurrences everywhere. The forces of good and evil are pitted against each other, and right seems mostly to prevail. (The ethical influence of Christianity might be seen here in the general triumph of right over wrong.) The stories abound with accounts of magical transformation: of people into animals or rich farmland into desert. The dead are resurrected in enchanted cauldrons; animals have the power of human speech; there are giants so large their bodies can span seas; and human heads are able survive decapitation and maintain their power to impart wisdom.

It is significant that the prominent women of Welsh myth are, for the most part, background players rather than actively heroic figures. They are nonetheless powerful characters, if only as enablers, instigators of war and peace. For instance, Branwen's wrongful treatment at the hands of her Irish husband leads to a disastrous

The Principal Welsh Gods and Heroes

Brân the Blessed (Bendigeidfran)	Divine lord of Harlech, Gwynedd
Branwen, sister of Brân	Catalyst for war between Wales and Ireland
Pwyll	Divine lord of Arberth (Narberth), Dyfed
Rhiannon, wife of Pwyll	A disguised horse-goddess
Pryderi, son of Pwyll and Rhiannon	Lord of Dyfed after his father
Manawydan	Enchanter, craftsman and god of farming
Math	Divine lord of Gwynedd and a creator god
Lleu Llaw Gyffes, son of Arianrhod	A god of light
Arianrhod, mother of Lleu	A moon-goddess
Arawn	God of the Otherworld (Annwfn)
Blodeuwedd	An amoral woman made from flowers
Mabon	A hunter-god
Gofannon	A smith-god
Rhonabwy	A hero of Powys
Peredur	A righter of wrongs and enemy of evil witches
Arthur	A hero of Britain
Culhwch	A divine hunter-hero and lover of Olwen
Olwen	Lover of Culhwch and daughter of the giant Ysbaddaden

conflict between Wales and Ireland that all but annihilated both. Rhiannon seems at first to be a robust and challenging character, an Otherworld goddess, able to confront the earthly power of Pwyll and to choose her own husband. But as the story develops (see pp. 81–83) she, like Branwen, becomes the archetypal 'calumniated wife' rather than a red-blooded mythic heroine. The only really robust 'woman' in the Mabinogion is Blodeuwedd, the wicked adulteress of the

Fourth Branch. Her powerful amorality is explained in terms of her not being truly human, conjured from flowers by magicians. The treatment of the women in Welsh mythology, perhaps more than any other features, betrays hidden Christian ideologies, in which women were for the most part unempowered appendages to men or helpless and hapless virgins (such as Goewin in the Fourth Branch) – or inhuman beings steeped in evil (such as Blodeuwedd).

● PWYLL AND RHIANNON ●

He took the horse and off he went. He came to the open level plain and showed his horse his spurs; and the more he pricked his horse, all the further was she from him. Yet she held to the same pace as that she had started with. His horse flagged, and when he knew of his horse that its speed was failing, he returned to where Pwyll was.

FROM THE FIRST BRANCH OF THE *MABINOGI*

The First Branch of the *Mabinogi* begins with a supernatural encounter between Pwyll, lord of Llys Arberth, and Arawn, king of the Otherworld. When both Pwyll and Arawn were out hunting one day, a dispute between them arose as to whose hounds had brought down the stag they were both pursuing. They settled their differences after Pwyll agreed to Arawn's request that they should exchange places for a year and a day, and that Pwyll should kill Arawn's rival Hafgan. Pwyll agreed, and spent an agreeable year feasting in Arawn's realm.

The account moves on to tell how Pwyll won his wife, Rhiannon, which was in a curious manner. She first appeared to him while he sat on a sacred mound (the *Gorsedd Arberth*), a dazzling gold-clad horsewoman riding a sparkling white horse that neither Pwyll nor his fleetest horseman could catch. She only stopped when he called out to her; their marriage soon followed.

The manner of their son Pryderi's birth and babyhood were steeped in Otherworld magic. First, Rhiannon did not conceive for three years after the marriage, and Pwyll's courtiers began to grumble at the absence of an heir, pressurizing Pwyll to put away his barren wife. Pwyll asked his men to grant them a year's grace before he divorced her and, lo and behold, in the true spirit of good

Gwawl and 'Badger in the Bag'

One day, when Pwyll and Rhiannon were celebrating their engagement at a feast, a young man appeared at Pwyll's hall, and was welcomed to join in the festivities. As was customary, he asked a favour of the lord, and Pwyll replied that he would give the stranger whatever he desired. The man asked for Rhiannon. It turned out that this traveller was none other than Gwawl, Rhiannon's rejected suitor. Rhiannon was furious, and Pwyll was in a quandary over what to do next, for he would be disgraced if he broke his word.

Rhiannon came up with an idea. She gave Pwyll a little bag, instructing him to keep it safely. She turned to Gwawl and told him to meet her in a year and a day's time when she would give a feast for him and then sleep with him. Pwyll was to be there when Gwawl claimed his bride, wearing ragged clothes and carrying the little bag. The day of the nuptials dawned. Gwawl appeared with his retinue, and Pwyll arrived with his bag. As had been planned, Pwyll asked Rhiannon to fill the bag with food, but however much was placed in it, the bag still had room.

Gwawl asked Rhiannon if the bag could ever be filled; she replied that only if a powerful lord jumped into the bag and trod down the contents. Gwawl immediately leapt into the bag and, quick as a flash, Pwyll closed the mouth of the bag, trapping his rival. He then sounded his horn to summon his men, and they all fell upon Gwawl's retinue and tied them up. As each of Pwyll's men entered the hall, he struck the bag a mighty blow, and asked what was inside. 'A badger' the others said, and so the game of 'Badger in the Bag' was created. After much discourse, Gwawl was released and slunk away to lick his wounds. That night, Pwyll and Rhiannon consummated their union.

storytelling, within that time Rhiannon bore a son. And then it all began to go badly wrong. On May-eve (always a dangerous time because it was the Celtic summer festival of Beltane) the new-born baby disappeared one night while the women detailed to watch over him were asleep. When they woke, they were so terrified of punishment for their dereliction of duty that they conspired to frame his mother Rhiannon, killing a puppy and smearing its blood on her hands and face so that she would take the blame – and not only for murder but for cannibalism too.

Despite being encouraged to execute his wife for her alleged horrific act, instead, Pwyll imposed a penance upon her that chimed with her affinity with horses, introduced (by the storyteller) when Rhiannon and Pwyll first met. Her punishment was that, for seven years, she had to act as if she were a beast of burden, sitting beside the horse-block by the gates of the court and bearing visitors to the king's palace on her back. Thus, the storyteller combined utter humiliation with a reminder to the audience of Rhiannon's horse-symbolism. The eventual resolution of the tale and vindication of Rhiannon is told below (see pp. 112–15).

• CREATION AND FALL •

All Four Branches of the *Mabinogi* are bristling with superhuman beings and events that oscillate between the great royal Welsh houses of Dyfed in the south and Gwynedd in the north. Tensions between the two unravel in the stories, and may well contain subtexts relating to genuine ancient conflicts between North and South Wales (rivalries that survive even today). It is not easy to disentangle the 'fairy-tale' aspects of the stories, with their messages of good and evil, pain and joy, from their essentially pagan divine structure. Who were the gods and who mere mortals, the playthings of veiled spirit-force?

It is the Fourth Branch that contains perhaps the most overtly pagan elements. A central character, Lleu Llaw Gyffes, son of Arianrhod, was given his name 'Bright One of the Skilful Hand' by his uncle Gwydion because his mother refused to name him. The name Lleu almost certainly betrays his origins as a god of light, like the Irish Lugh (both Lleu and Lugh were also craft-gods). This Fourth Branch also provides the closest thing to an origin myth found anywhere within the Welsh tradition, that of King Math of Gwynedd and his foot-holder.

The Virgin and the King

At that time Math, son of Mathonwy, could not live unless his feet were in the lap of a virgin, except when the turmoil of war prevented him. The maiden who was with him was Goewin daughter of Pebin from Dol Pebin in Arfon. And she was the fairest maiden of her generation known at the time.
FROM THE FOURTH BRANCH OF THE *MABINOGI*

The Fourth Branch pivots upon the towering figure of Math, Lord of Gwynedd, son of Mathonwy. Math was almost certainly of divine origin. His story is distinctive in Welsh mythology because it may reflect a pre-Christian myth of Creation and Fall. A condition of Math's power – and indeed his life – was that, unless he was away fighting his enemies, he must stay at home and, bizarrely, sit with his feet in the lap of a maiden: the girl's virginity was imperative. The name of Math's foot-holder was Goewin. This strange prohibition on Math's rule can best be explained if his origins lay in the pagan mythic tradition of sacral kingship so prevalent in Irish myths, wherein the mortal king 'married' the land in the form of the goddess of sovereignty. In a Welsh twist, the virgin status of the 'goddess' appears to reflect the perceived power of undissipated female sexuality, whose concentrated potency was necessary for the land to remain prosperous.

But the connection between royal feet and the land may have even more complex roots. When Captain Cook explored Tahiti in the mid-18th century, he came across a tradition in which a Polynesian chieftain journeying outside his own lands had to be carried because any territory on which he set foot automatically became his, thus risking war between him and neighbouring chiefdoms. Clearly it would be outrageous to suppose direct connections between early medieval Wales and 18th-century Polynesia. But Cook's observations inspire us to look for deeper ways of interpreting Math's situation.

The audience listening to this orally transmitted tale would know right from the start that this peculiar condition of Math's reign over Gwynedd was almost bound to be broken, and so it was. His nephew Gilfaethwy lusted after Goewin and conspired with his brother Gwydion to foment conflict away from Gwynedd and so cause Math to be absent from his court and his foot-holder. Gwydion initiated a war between Gwynedd and Dyfed to the south by mentioning to Math that Pryderi, Lord of Dyfed, possessed some special new animals, pigs, which had never been seen in the North and whose flesh was reputedly sweeter than that of beef. They came from Annwfn, the Otherworld, and were a present from its lord Arawn. Math wanted them, and sent Gwydion to get them. Now Gwydion was a magician, who could charm almost anything out of anyone by means of his gift of storytelling. He went as a friend to Pryderi's court but then stole the pigs by trickery. War ensued: Gwydion's forces prevailed and Pryderi was killed.

When Math returned home, he found that his virgin foot-holder was virgin no longer: Gilfaethwy had raped her, thus disempowering the king. Math retaliated by turning the two brothers into wild animals. Math immediately dismissed the now useless Goewin, marrying her off to a nobleman at his court, and advertised for a replacement. One candidate, Arianrhod ('Silver Wheel'), came forward. She had to pass a test of virginity, by stepping over Math's magic staff. Sadly, she failed abysmally: as she stepped over the wand, she gave birth to twins. One, Dylan, took to the sea and passed out of myth; the second was taken and fostered by Gwydion. The storyteller fails to say whether or not Math ever managed to recruit a new foot-holder. If he was unsuccessful, the inference is that his power was diminished.

In her shame at having failed her virginity test, Arianrhod utterly repudiated her second son. She laid a curse upon him that he would have no name unless she chose to name him herself; that he would never bear arms unless she herself were to arm him; and that he would never have a wife. Gwydion, the child's uncle, got round all these prohibitions by means of magic. So Arianrhod's second son was named Lleu Llaw Gyffes. To overcome the third of his mother's prohibitions, Lleu obtained a magical wife, conjured from flowers by Gwydion. Her name was Blodeuwedd ('Flower Woman'). But she was faithless and conspired to murder her husband (see pp. 135–37).

Mortally wounded by a spear-thrust from Blodeuwedd's lover Gronw, Lleu gave a great screech, turned into an eagle and flew into an oak-tree, where Gwydion eventually found him, led to the spot by a sow that fed beneath it (pigs again!).

● THE GOLDEN BOWL AND THE SPELLBOUND LAND ●

And on the edge of the fountain a golden bowl fastened to four chains, and that upon a marble slab, and the chains ascending into the air, and he could see no end of them. He was transported with the great beauty of the gold and with the exceeding good workmanship of the bowl, and he came to where the bowl was and laid hold of it. And as soon as he laid hold of the bowl, his two hands stuck to the bowl, and his feet to the slab on which he was standing, and all his power of speech forsook him, so that he could not utter one word.

FROM THE THIRD BRANCH OF THE *MABINOGI*

Manawydan son of Llyr, principal protagonist of the Third Branch, was of the royal Welsh house of Dyfed and brother to Brân and Branwen. Like his Irish divine counterpart Manannán mac Lir, Manawydan was a magician and a trickster. He also had a consummate skill as a craftsman. He married Rhiannon, heroine of the First Branch, after the death of her first husband Pwyll. Another link between the two Branches was the *Gorsedd Arberth*. In the First Branch, this special place granted Pwyll his first sighting of Rhiannon. But Manawydan's encounter with the *Gorsedd* revealed catastrophe. He and his new wife went up to the mound with Pryderi, his stepson, and Pryderi's wife Cigfa. As they did so, a spell was cast on the land of Dyfed, which simply disappeared: nothing was left to see but mist.

The four decided to travel to England to seek their fortune, leaving the void of Dyfed behind. When they reached a town, the two men set up shop as smiths, cobblers or saddlers, but they were so good at their trades that they took everyone else's business and were driven out by their furious competitors. So, hounded from England, they all returned to where Dyfed had been, and survived by hunting. But the Otherworld was never far away. During one hunting expedition, Manawydan and Pryderi encountered a supernatural boar, immense and dazzling white (like Rhiannon's white horse), which enticed the hunters and their hounds to a strange castle. Manawydan held back, suspicious of the place, but, despite the warnings of his companion, Pryderi insisted on following the animal into the castle. Inside, the first thing he saw was a gleaming golden bowl suspended from the ceiling with chains. As he touched it, an enchantment fell on him so that he could neither move nor speak. His mother Rhiannon heard what had happened, followed him into the castle and was similarly spellbound.

Manawydan could no longer hunt, for his dogs had disappeared with Pryderi, so he turned to farming and began to grow wheat. This part of the myth might be a remnant of an ancient origin tale that sought to explain how arable farming was introduced into Wales (just as the theft of Pryderi's supernatural pigs by Gwydion may be a mythic tale to explain the introduction of pig-farming). Just when Manawydan was about to gather in the harvest, two of his fields were devastated by a plague of mice.

He lay in wait for them to attack the next field but they were too fast for him, all except a pregnant one, too slow to escape. In a bizarre punishment scene, he attempted to hang the mouse, but was interrupted by a bishop who tried to prevent her death. Manawydan recognized the 'bishop' as a fellow magician, who had blighted Dyfed with evil spells because of an ancient grievance against Rhiannon and her first husband Pwyll. The 'mouse' was his wife. Manawydan bargained with him for her life, demanding the restoration of Dyfed and the release of Pryderi and Rhiannon from the enchanted bowl. In return, Manawydan spared the 'mouse', who returned to her human form.

● MAGIC BOWLS ●

What was the significance of the golden bowl that cast a binding-spell on Pryderi and Rhiannon? Bowls, dishes and drinking-cups of precious metal were important symbols of prosperity and, perhaps, of religious function, throughout the early Iron Age and the early Christian period in Britain and Europe. At one end of the spectrum is the sheet-gold bowl from Zürich Altstetten, made in the 6th century BC. The vessel was decorated with a frieze of deer, hares and alternating full and crescent moons. It must surely have been a ceremonial object, used by clergy in ritual activities, perhaps associated with night.

At the other end of the chronological timeline is the splendid silver, gold-inlaid Irish Christian chalice made in about 700 and found in Ardagh, Co. Limerick. Bowls like these, whether pagan

Chased gold bowl, 6th century BC, from Zürich Altstetten, decorated with hares, deer and moons.

The silver Ardagh Chalice, c. AD 700, bears the names of the apostles alongside elaborate Celtic designs with animal ornaments.

or Christian, represent not only drinking but also transformation. Liquor is the juice of fruit or grain transformed into an alcoholic drink. According to Christian tradition, a chalice holds the wine that becomes Christ's blood during the Eucharist. The Christian writer recording the Welsh mythic tales may well have had gold and silver chalices in mind when he wrote of the magical vessel that entranced Pryderi and Rhiannon. If so, the tale is a wonderful amalgam of pagan and Christian tradition, where enchanted animals erupt from

The Holy Grail

An iconic and enduring feature of medieval Celtic literature is the story of the Holy Grail. The Grail legends did not originate in Wales, but in France. The earliest account, by Chrétien de Troyes, dates to around 1180. The Grail story is principally a 'quest tale'. It is just one of the French Arthurian Romances. The main character was Perceval, an Arthurian knight who, while out wandering in the wilderness, encountered a lame old man who invited him to his castle. During dinner there, Perceval witnessed a weird procession, led by a squire carrying a lance dripping with blood, followed by a beautiful young girl bearing a jewelled cup or dish, called a *graal*. After her came candle-bearers and a group of courtiers clad in mourning clothes.

Too polite to enquire of what he had seen, Perceval went to bed and rose the next morning to find the castle deserted. He continued his travels, but along the way he met a young woman who rebuked him for not asking about the procession he had seen at the castle. This encounter threw Perceval into an agony of doubt and longing, and he began the long quest to find the castle again and discover the secret of the grail.

Other medieval French authors took up Chrétien's grail story and embellished it so that it became tangled up with Joseph of Arimathea: the bleeding lance had once belonged to Longinus, the Roman soldier present at the Crucifixion, and the grail the cup used by Joseph to collect Christ's blood. According to one branch of the legend, the grail was identified as the cup used by Christ at the Last Supper.

the Otherworld to entice humans back with them and 'Christian' church plate was thrown into the mix in order to convey a half-hidden subtext of Christian power.

● WALES *VS* IRELAND: THE WAR OF THE WORLDS ●

Archaeological evidence points to strong connections between Ireland and the west of Britain from early prehistory onwards. Welsh mythology makes recurrent references to links with Ireland that were not always friendly. One of the most cataclysmic events to be described in the Four Branches of the *Mabinogi* was the great war between Wales and Ireland, a conflict that all but destroyed both countries.

A function of myth is to explain the origins of alliances and confrontations between self-determined communities. In early medieval Hiberno-British society, the Irish Sea acted to connect rather than divide the lands on its borders. But sharing this 'Celtic Pond' clearly had the potential for tensions as well as for treaties of friendship, particularly if rival groups were vying for land, fish or mineral resources. The principal focus of the Second Branch of the Mabinogion is a quarrel between King Brân of Harlech in North Wales and King Matholwch of Ireland over the latter's betrothal to Brân's sister Branwen. The beginning of the story seems somewhat contrived to suggest tension since, although the Irish king was making a journey to Wales in order to ask for Branwen's hand in marriage, the appearance of his 13 ships off the north Welsh coast seem to come as a total surprise to the Harlech court. Indeed, when the flotilla is first sighted, Brân and his men think they represent an enemy invasion and arm themselves ready to defend their land.

Matholwch assures Brân that he has come in friendship and seeks to marry Branwen. Her brother agrees and everyone, Welsh and Irish alike, sets off to Aberffraw on the island of Anglesey, the chief seat of the lords of Gwynedd. Perhaps this place had been chosen as a ceremonial centre because of its position, on an island on the very edge of Britain: it is isolated, with a savagely rugged coastline, separated from the mainland by a narrow band of water beset by vicious currents, and accessible only to flat-bottomed ships or small boats.

Once all the courtiers of the two lands had assembled, a great cele-bratory feast began. The banquets had to take place in tents, though, because Brân was too large to fit inside any building.

But disaster was soon to spoil the merrymaking, when Branwen's brother Efnisien savagely maimed Matholwch's horses in his anger at the betrothal. The only gift that would mollify Branwen's would-be bridegroom was Brân's most valuable possession, his cauldron of rebirth. The marriage thus took place and Branwen set sail for her new Irish home. But Matholwch's insult had been neither forgiven nor forgotten and Branwen suffered severe ill-treatment at the Irish court. Hearing of his sister's plight, Brân declared war on Ireland. Cauldrons could be capricious things. Matholwch used Brân's life-regenerating vessel against him. Every night, Irish soldiers killed in battle were immersed in the cauldron and emerged fighting-fit, ready to return to the fray. But they were zombies, undead bodies who were unable to speak, or to do anything but fight.

Finally, the fate of Efnisien, the instigator of all the trouble, and the cauldron came together: he leaped inside, killing himself and causing the vessel to shatter into four pieces. Branwen was broken-hearted by all that had happened, blaming herself for the carnage. She died on the banks of the river Alaw near Holyhead, where she could look upon her marital homeland from that of her birth.

In Ireland, the only people left alive after the slaughter by the Welsh were five pregnant women in a cave. They each gave birth to a baby boy at exactly the same time. When the children grew up, they each had sex with another's mother and divided the land into five plots, and these became the five medieval provinces of Ireland. The five men scoured the land for the spoils of long-gone battles and became rich with the gold and silver they found. Maybe this particular story relates to the discovery in medieval times of some of the rich gold objects known from Bronze and Iron Age Ireland.

• PEREDUR AND THE WITCH •

'There are nine witches here, friend,' the lady said to Peredur,
'together with their father and mother. They are the witches of
Caerloyw. And by daybreak we shall be no nearer to making
our escape than to being killed. And they have taken over and
laid waste the land, except for this one house.'
FROM 'PEREDUR'

The young hero Peredur was the seventh son of Earl Efrog (the name is that of ancient York, and Efrog is credited as the founder of the medieval city). Peredur is probably the same character as Perceval in Chrétien de Troyes's Arthurian Grail Romance. Efrog and six of his sons were killed in battle; the only survivor was Peredur. In the Welsh tale, his mother sought to preserve his life and so she took him and hid him in the wilderness. While out wandering one day, the young man encountered some of Arthur's knights. When he told his mother of this, she told him to go to Arthur's court. After many setbacks and bouts of single combat with noblemen, Peredur arrived at the court of Arthur at Caerleon.

A recurrent theme of the Peredur story is the neverending tussle between good and evil. The most vivid representation of the latter is embodied by the Nine Witches of Caerloyw (Gloucester). Indeed, an underlying ribbon of meaning in 'Peredur' is the links it makes between different parts of Britain: northern England, the West Country and southeast Wales. Peredur received a warning from a lady against the Nine Witches: these inimical women had laid waste all the land surrounding her castle. At dawn on the day after the warning, Peredur encountered one of the witches as she attacked the castle watch-keeper. The hero intervened and struck her on the head. The witch recognized him, hailing him by name and predicting her destiny to be injured by him. She went on to advise him that she should instruct him in the craft of war. Such military training by a woman is highly reminiscent of the Ulster hero Cú Chulainn's

Peredur comes to the aid of a watchman, who is being strangled by one of the Nine Witches of Caerloyw.

The Number Nine in Welsh Myth

Peredur's Nine Witches present one of many occasions in Celtic mythology where numbers, particularly three (see pp. 30–33) and its multiples, were highly charged with supernatural significance. The association between otherworldly females and the number nine is a persistent one. Arthur's excursion to Annwfn (the Welsh Otherworld), as chronicled in 'The Spoils of Annwfn', involves an encounter with nine sacred virgins who tended the magical cauldron that Arthur sought to steal. More than a thousand years earlier, the Roman author Pomponius Mela wrote of another set of nine virgin priestesses, who inhabited one of the Scilly Isles, off the far west tip of Cornwall. These women served a famous oracle and they themselves also possessed the power to tell the future, cure the sick and even control the sea, wind and weather.

tutelage in battle skills by Scáthach, whose name, 'Shadowy One', proclaims her supernatural status (see pp. 106–8). Like Peredur's witches, Scáthach, too, was a seer. Peredur exacted from the witch the promise that the lady of the castle's lands should be harmed no more. He then lived with the Nine Witches for three weeks receiving tuition in war-craft from them.

Some time later, the hero found out that the witches had been active again, this time attacking Peredur's own family, killing a cousin and maiming an uncle. Peredur enlisted the help of Arthur and a fellow-knight Gwalchmai, taking a band of warriors to fight the witches. The women prophesied that Peredur and his army would destroy them, and so it transpired. The Caerloyw witches appear to have had exactly the same functions as the Irish battle-furies, the Badbh and the Morrigán: they were prophetesses, associated with battle, intensely destructive; and their destiny was tightly bound up with young heroes in a dichotomous relationship between good and evil.

• THE ENIGMA OF ARTHUR •

'Go thy way,' said she, 'to Arthur's court, where are the best of men and the most generous and bravest. Wherever thou seest a church, recite thy pater thereto. If you see meat and drink, shouldst thou be in need thereof and it not be given thee of courtesy and good will, take it thyself. If thou hear an outcry, make towards it, and a woman's outcry above any cry in the world.'

FROM 'PEREDUR'

Arthur is a persistently iconic figure in medieval myths and histories. In the Welsh myths, he is associated with a curious mix of Christianity and pagan magic. God is frequently mentioned, but rubs shoulders with enchanted animals and magic cauldrons. Arthur's

Arthur and the Dream of Rhonabwy

The Welsh mythic tale known as 'The Dream of Rhonabwy' dates to the 13th century in its written form. It concerns the kingdom of Powys and its ruler Madawg, whose brother Iorwoerth, a troublemaker, sought to overthrow the rightful ruler by harrying the countryside and its people. Madawg called upon his followers to seek him out, and one of these was Rhonabwy. As its name indicates, the story is woven around a dream this man had, when asleep lying on an ox-skin during battle, in which he saw a complex vision.

Arthur was a prominent person in the dream, and is referred to as the emperor of Britain, whose enmity with one Iddawg, the 'Embroiler of Britain', led to the Battle of Camlann in about AD 540. (This battle between the Christian British and the pagan Saxons is known historically, from the *Easter Annals*.) One of the supernatural features of the 'Dream' is the magical raven army of Owein that fought against Arthur's warriors while the two men were playing the ancient board game of *gwyddbwyll*. The raven-soldiers got the upper hand, but peace was made between the two. As the game came to an end, Rhonabwy woke from his dream, having slept for three days and nights.

name is associated with several sites, including Caerleon (its Roman amphitheatre was imagined as being the original Round Table), the Celtic monastery at Tintagel in Cornwall and Glastonbury Abbey in Somerset. Many place names claim association: from Arthur's Stone, a Neolithic chambered tomb in Herefordshire, to Arthur's Seat, an Iron Age hillfort in Edinburgh. The main Arthurian stories are contained in the medieval French Romances, principally those compiled by Chrétien de Troyes in the late 12th century. But Arthur is mentioned in a number of Welsh mythological tales, including 'Culhwch and Olwen' and 'Peredur'. He is always presented as a larger-than-life, heroic figure, a champion fighter surrounded by gallant knights.

In the early historical sources, such as Nennius's 9th-century *Historia Brittonum*, Arthur is presented as a defender of Britain against foreign invaders, whether from the north, west or east. As an historical figure, his most significant victory was against the English at Mount Badon near Bath in the early 6th century. He was neither a king nor the founder of a dynasty. He was a war-leader, the head of a group of small kingdoms that emerged in Britain in the aftermath of its separation from the Roman Empire in the early 5th century. The legends that clustered around Arthur are much more significant than the man himself. The living historical figure of Arthur inspired a whole constellation of stories about medieval chivalry, heroism and consummate fighting skill that spanned not only Wales but also the whole of Britain and beyond.

Reconstruction of the Roman amphitheatre at Caerleon, Wales, as it might have looked in the late 1st or early 2nd century AD.

THE CHAMPION'S PORTION:
MYTHICAL HEROES

When a large number dine together they sit round in a circle
with the most influential man in the centre … whether he
surpass the others in warlike skill, or nobility of family, or
wealth…. When the hindquarters were served up the bravest
hero took the thigh piece, and if another man claimed it they
stood up and fought in single combat to the death.
ATHENAEUS IV

In the 3rd century AD, the Greek writer Athenaeus recorded a range
of customs that used to be followed by the Gauls, not least the importance of feasting, and of choosing communal meal-times to honour
their greatest warriors. The focus of these banquets was meat, which,
according to the earlier writer Diodorus, was boiled in cauldrons
and roasted on spits. Alcoholic drink was passed round in a shared
tankard from man to man, but the supreme champion was always
honoured with the best portion of meat. People ate the meat by
grasping huge lumps of it in both hands and biting off large chunks.

Two elements of these Classical authors' comments are significant to Celtic myth: communal eating and drinking, and the
'champion's portion'. Both themes play important roles in Irish and
Welsh mythic literature, and the excessive consumption of both
meat – particularly pork – and liquor are associated with the Welsh
and Irish Otherworlds. Even more importantly, the selection and
support of an Irish king were dependent upon his generosity to his
people and his ability to provide largesse to his noblemen. One king,
Bres, failed miserably: his meanness was legendary and was allegedly
the direct cause of crop-failure, an indication that Ireland herself had
turned her back on him and had withdrawn sovereignty from him.

• POWER-DRINKING IN THE EUROPEAN IRON AGE •

Taken to excess, alcohol, like any psychotropic drug, can bend minds and induce 'out-of-body' experiences. In later prehistoric Europe, drinking appears to be especially associated with funerary rituals and ceremonial occasions, perhaps because it was deemed a means of making contact with the world of the spirits. Throughout the British and European Iron Age, there was a persistent habit of burying the elite dead with eating and drinking equipment, not just for one individual but for dinner-parties, similar to the *symposia*, the all-male drinking clubs of ancient Greece. The tomb of a chieftain who died around 550 BC at Hochdorf in Germany contained a couch on which the body lay, together with a dinner service for nine and a large Greek cauldron that had contained 300 litres (66 gallons) of mead. Nine drinking horns were hung on the walls of the grave and the chieftain's own horn, placed above his head, held a massive 5.5 litres (10 pints) of liquor.

Groups of high-status cremation burials in southeast England and northern Gaul exhibit the recurrent preoccupation with funerary feasting. There, the emphasis was on Mediterranean wine, and amphorae (ceramic vessels for the shipment of wine) were placed in tombs, along with goblets, wine-strainers, jars for olive oil and cylindrical buckets containing local liquor, such as ale or fermented berry-juices. The purpose of interring such material was to emphasize the importance of liquor-consumption on a lavish scale, and perhaps the focus of such funerals was to communicate with the gods and thus ease the rite of passage for the deceased so that the soul could enter the Otherworld without hindrance.

The Iron Age evidence for large-scale feasting is also reflected in early Ireland. Finely made drinking-cups, such as one from Keshcarrigan in Co. Leitrim, with its exquisite bird's head handle, might belong to the Iron Age or early Christian period, and were clearly for more important occasions than everyday domestic use.

The great tankard from Carrickfergus in Co. Antrim, like its late Iron Age fellows from Wales, was designed for passing round a shared drink, much as described by Diodorus. Perhaps drinking-vessels like these were used in communal religious events and then may have been too greatly charged with sanctity or spirit-force to remain in circulation, so were given honourable burial in wetland (water was thought to be a gateway between the worlds of people and the spirits). But what greater statement about the importance of feasting could be found than the huge 12th-century bronze-bound Irish drinking horn known as the Kavanagh Charter Horn, which would be used, 300 years later, as grounds for legitimizing a claim to rule the kingdom of Leinster?

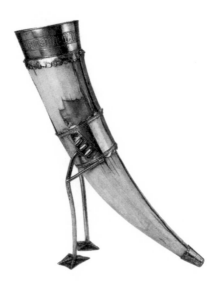

The Kavanagh Horn, used in the inauguration ceremony for King Kavanagh of Leinster, Ireland. 12th century AD.

• THE OTHERWORLD FEAST •

Mac Da Thó's pig was slaughtered for the feast. This pig had been nourished by sixty milch cows for seven years, and it was brought into the feast with forty oxen laid across it.
FROM THE *TÁIN BÓ CUAILNGE*

Irish and Welsh mythology contains constant references to a Happy Otherworld of ceaseless feasting and hunting. In Ireland, the nuclei of the feast were ever-replenishing cooking-cauldrons and self-regenerating pigs. Each deity had his or her own hostel of *sídh*, and in each one feasting was central. One Irish story, 'Da Derga's Hostel', paints a chilling picture of a 'hog-roast', where the same pig was slaughtered and eaten each day, only to be reborn and killed anew; here, the lord of the feast is described as a man carrying a pig over his shoulder, ready-cooked but still squealing. He appeared to Conaire, an Ulster king, as a monstrous man with one eye, one hand and one foot, with shins as thick as yokes and buttocks the size of enormous cheeses, all these bodily deviances marking him as belonging to the Otherworld.

A story in the Ulster Cycle, called 'Mac Da Thó's Pig', is specifically about the Champion's Portion of pork, used as a focus in the intense enmity between Ulster and Connacht. Mac Da Thó was a king of Leinster who possessed a huge hound that was coveted by the people of both provinces. The king promised to make a gift of the dog to both the Ulstermen and the Connachtmen. When they both came to claim the animal, the Leinster king invited them to attend a feast at his great hall, the centrepiece of which was a gigantic roasting pig. Squabbles broke out between the warriors of Ulster and Connacht over who should be presented with the Champion's Portion, and Mac Da Thó let loose his hound to see which side it supported: the dog chose the Ulstermen and the men of Connacht were defeated. Given that the tale was part of the Ulster Cycle, the outcome is hardly surprising.

Enchanted Pigs

The Biblical New Testament story of the Gadarene swine is a tale of possession. When Jesus cast out a 'legion' of devils from a sick man, he sent the evil spirits into a herd of swine, which then rampaged and hurled themselves over a cliff to their destruction. As we shall see in Chapter 6, the theme of enchanted pigs is a common one in Celtic myths and this is likely to have been because pork was a symbolic and high-status food and because wild boar were thought the bravest of animals.

The emphasis on pork in the Irish mythic tales corresponds with its appearance in the British and European Iron Age archaeological record as high-status meat. Joints of pork were frequently placed with the dead among grave goods whose richness points to the high rank of the dead person. One distinctive group of tombs are the so-called 'chariot-burials' of the middle later Iron Age, found mostly in East Yorkshire and in the Marne region of eastern France. Features of these graves include the inhumed burial of a man or woman together with a light, two-wheeled cart, entire or dismantled, metal grave goods, including weapons or personal items, and the remains of sides of pork.

Late Iron Age stone figure of a man wearing a torc (neckring), with a wild boar striding along his torso.

The reverence and assumption of wild boars' bravery is demonstrated by the use of the boar as a badge by Iron Age warriors, who wore the symbol on helmets and shields when going into battle. During the 1st century BC, someone made an offering, perhaps to the gods of victory, in the Lincolnshire river Witham, of a shield emblazoned with a fantastic image of a boar. War-trumpets, called *carnyces*, their mouths in the form of boars' heads, were carried into battle, making such a fearsome and confusing racket that Classical writers commented that this psychological warfare on the battlefield was almost as effective as a weapon.

Feasting had its place in the Welsh Otherworld, too. The most vivid account appears in the First Branch of the *Mabinogi*, when Pwyll, the heroic lord of Dyfed, changed places with Arawn, king of the Otherworld for a year and a day. When Pwyll arrived, he found the most lavish court he had ever seen, with great halls, squires to wait on him, Arawn's queen dressed in rich golden brocaded silk, jewelled knights and ladies and tables, groaning with food and drink the lavishness of which he had never before encountered. Pwyll spent his year in hunting, carousing, singing and conversation.

• THE CELTIC HERO •

Heroes are central to myth because they are superhuman, semi-divine and bridge the divide between the material world and that of the spirits. Such hybrid, edgy, 'liminal' characters are both immensely powerful, but also vulnerable, because they belong in neither camp and the gods cannot resist meddling with them, often using them in tugs-of-war for divine supremacy. We see this in Classical mythology in the treatment of 'big men', such as Achilles, Hercules and Aeneas.

In Celtic mythology, heroes – almost all male – were the epitome, the Platonic ideal, of masculine virtues. Some, like the Welsh Brân, were giants; others, of whom the Ulster hero Cú Chulainn is the most prominent, had superhuman qualities as a warrior, even during an abnormally precocious childhood.

Heroes and Single Combat

He towers on the battlefield
in breastplate and red cloak.
Across the sinister chariot-wheel;
the Warped Man deals death....
Whole hosts he will destroy,
making dense massacre.
In thousands you will yield your heads.
I am Fedelm. I hide nothing.
FROM THE *TÁIN BÓ CUAILNGE*

So did the prophetess Fedelma warn Medbh of the single-handed prowess in battle of Ulster's hero Cú Chulainn (see below). The centrepiece of the Ulster mythic prose tales is the *Táin Bó Cuailnge*, the saga of warfare between the great Irish states of Ulster, whose king was Conchobar, and Connacht (Connaught), ruled by Queen Medbh. The longstanding conflict between the two flared into life over rivalry between two great bulls, the Donn (Brown) Bull of Ulster and Finnbhennach, the 'white-horned' bull of Connacht. Although Medbh's bull was renowned for his courage and mettle, she coveted the Donn and tried to 'borrow' him. When the Ulstermen refused, the queen assembled a great army to invade Ulster and steal the Donn, and the great war began. The Ulstermen were at a disadvantage because of a curse that made them as weak as women in labour. The only man exempt from this scourge was Cú Chulainn, and he, superhuman hero that he was, took on the might of Connacht single-handed, helped by his divine avatar, the battle-goddess Badbh. The two bulls also fought each other: the Donn of Ulster slew Medbh's white-horned bull, but then also died of exhaustion.

Single combat and the individual hero are common tropes in myth: witness the battle between Achilles and Hector outside the gates of Troy, and David and the giant Philistine Goliath in the

Biblical Old Testament. In describing how battles were fought amongst the Iron Age Gauls in the 1st century BC, Classical writers refer to just this form of military foreplay: the battle-lines would be drawn up and each side would put forward a hero to fight in single combat. Sometimes this would not develop beyond boasting and strutting, showing off fine armour, sabre-rattling and exchanges of belligerent words. But if physical combat did take place, its outcome often decided victory or defeat with no general bloodshed. The role of the hero as a battle-champion was thus supremely important for communities not only for status but also in helping to avoid squandering limited manpower.

• CÚ CHULAINN: CULANN'S HOUND •

'Until that hound grows up to do his work, I will be your hound, and guard yourself and your beasts. And I will guard all Murtheimne Plain. No flock or herd will leave my care unknown to me.'
'Cúchulainn shall be your name, the Hound of Culann,'
Cathbad said.
FROM THE *TÁIN BÓ CUAILNGE*

The supreme Ulster hero, Cú Chulainn is depicted as larger than life and of supernatural status. His paternity was uncertain, but he was probably the son of Lugh, god of light and crafts. As befits such a giant among mortals, his childhood was marked by momentous acts, such that when only five years old he routed 50 of King Conchobar's youth brigade singlehanded. While he was still a child, he demanded to be given arms and become a fully fledged warrior; after shattering 15 sets of weapons, he finally accepted those belonging to the king himself, but not before they had been reinforced to make them strong enough to withstand the vigour of their new infant owner. Cú Chulainn's extreme precocity was also indicated by his physical appearance. Not only was he dazzlingly beautiful, but he also had bodily deviances: triple-coloured hair, seven pupils in each eye and seven fingers and toes on each hand and foot.

The term 'Cú' is Irish for dog, and it was often used as a form of privileged title for particularly valorous and skilful fighters. Cú Chulainn's given name was Sétanta, but he acquired his sobriquet in a curious manner. During his boyhood, he slew the hound of Culann the Smith, and, as a self-imposed penance, he promised to act in the dog's place and guard the smithy, even to the extent of naming himself as Culann's hound.

This association was to prove Cú Chulainn's downfall for, because of his pledge, a *geis* or prohibition was imposed on him never to partake of dog-meat. Breaking a *geis* usually spelled personal disaster and, indeed, towards the end of the hero's life, he was forced to break it in order to avoid breaking another taboo, that of refusing hospitality. On this occasion, he was served with dog-meat when a guest at a meal, and so he was faced with a double-bind from which it was impossible to escape. Having eaten the meat offered to him, his fate was set: not long afterwards, he was killed in battle.

Cú Chulainn's affinity with animals marked him out as a supernatural hero. As well as dogs, horses were a key association. Two foals were born at exactly the same moment as the hero, and they grew up with him to become his chariot-horses. They were named the Grey of Macha and the Black of Saingliu. Their fates were inextricably intertwined with his own: before his final, fatal battle, the Grey wept tears of blood.

Scáthach's Training

The young Cú Chulainn was instructed in war-craft by a woman called Scáthach, whose name means 'She Who Walks in Shadow'. Not only a fearsome battle trainer, she was also a seer who could use her powers in divination to predict future events. Her teaching was so superb that she turned Cú Chulainn into a fighting machine that

Divine Hound-Lords in Roman Britain

A deity worshipped in a shrine at Nettleton Shrub in Wiltshire was called Apollo Cunomaglus, 'the Hound-Lord'. An anonymous hunter-god from Southwark in London is depicted on a stone carving standing between two large hounds. These are but two of many local deities associated with the hunt in Roman Britain. The dogs appear to have been central to their cult, and it seems possible that the affinity between dogs and deities presented in this evidence perhaps fed in some way into the Cú Chulainn myth.

Romano-British carving of a hunter-god, from Southwark, London.

According to many hunting traditions, the hunter was special, someone who needed to be set apart from others, and keep himself pure and celibate before the hunt. The relationship between hunter and hunted was also complex. Respect needed to be shown to hunted prey; otherwise the herds of game would not return to be hunted afresh. So the hunt encapsulated intricate and apparently contradictory connections between its participants. In a way, the hunting-dog could be perceived as a go-between, just as the spirit packs of dogs in Welsh myth enabled transference between the material realms and the spirit-world. Cú Chulainn himself, as a half-human half-divine hero, also fulfilled this role as a conduit between layers of the cosmos.

no one could beat. Scáthach lived 'in the land of Alba' (all we know of this place is that it was somewhere to the east of Ulster, perhaps in Scotland). When the young hero travelled there, her pupils directed him to an island, reached by a bridge that nobody could cross unless already trained in war-craft. Three times Cú Chulainn tried to walk over the bridge and three times the far end of the bridge tipped up and threw him on his back. Finally, Cú Chulainn went berserk and ran so fast over the bridge that it could not unbalance him.

Scáthach's beautiful daughter Uathach met the Ulster hero at the gate. She informed him that if he really was keen to learn heroic deeds he must leap into a big yew tree where her mother rested, put his sword between her breasts and make her promise him three things: thorough training, a marriage dowry and the telling of his future. He did this and Scáthach took him as her pupil.

The Berserk Hero

The first warp-spasm seized Cú Chulainn, and made him into a monstrous thing, hideous and shapeless, unheard of. His shanks and his joints, every knuckle and angle and organ from head to foot, shook like a tree in the flood or a reed in the stream. His body made a furious twist inside his skin, so that his feet and shins and knees switched to the rear and his heels and calves switched to the front.
FROM THE *TÁIN BÓ CUAILNGE*

Although the Irish mythic stories are peppered with heroes, Cú Chulainn was the only one who regularly went into 'warp-spasm', a kind of maniacal overdrive in battle that allowed him to kill huge numbers of enemy soldiers. But warp-spasm rendered the hero so insane that he could not discriminate between his own side and his opponents. A charming tale associated with this insensate slaughter tells how, on one occasion, the Ulstermen were so frightened by Cú Chulainn's berserk killing-spree that they sent a group of

Cú Chulainn's Magical Weapons

As befitted a supernatural hero, the Ulster champion had special weapons and armour to help him overcome his enemies. The most dreadful was the *Gae Bulga*, a spear whose barbs always proved fatal to anyone injured by it. The sea-god Manannán gave him a visor to protect his face, and Cú Chulainn's chariot-driver could cast an invisible cloak over the chariot, its occupants and its horses.

Iron Age iron spearhead inlaid with gold, from the Thames in London.

naked women to him in the hope that his embarrassment at seeing them would calm him down. But when this failed, it was clear that something more drastic was needed to bring the hero out of his war-madness. The Ulstermen decided to cool him down in a cauldron, though it took three vessels of icy water to do so: the first cauldron burst from the heat of his body; in the second the water bubbled and seethed; only the water in the third managed to cool him sufficiently to end his berserk state.

Warp-spasm had terrifying physical effects: the hero's body became distorted and revolved in its skin; his hair stood on end, with a nimbus of light surrounding his head; his muscles swelled as though they would burst from his body; one eye bulged from his face while the other sank deep into the skull; his lips curled so far back that his throat was clearly visible; his great war-cry summoned up the spirits, who all howled with him and drove his enemies mad with fear.

Touched by the Gods: Cú Chulainn and the Supernatural

*A chariot was given to him. He clapped his hand to the chariot
between the shafts, and the frame broke at his touch. In the
same way he broke twelve chariots. At last they gave the boy
King Conchobar's chariot and that survived him.*
FROM THE *TÁIN BÓ CUAILNGE*

Cú Chulainn's supernatural status was flagged up by further storytelling devices, particularly prophecies of his heroic deeds, and the
intimate relationships he had with divine figures. During the Ulster
hero's boyhood, when he demanded to be allowed to bear arms, the
Druid Cathbad predicted that whoever took up arms on that day
would have a brief but glorious life. When war was brewing between
Connacht and Ulster, the prophetess Fedelma correctly prophesied
to Queen Medbh that her kingdom would be defeated by a blond
man, with the hero-light shining round his head, his lips drawn
back in a snarl, with many-pupilled eyes and that Connacht would
dissolve in a sea of bloodshed.

Throughout his life, Cú Chulainn was both plagued and aided
by gods and goddesses. When he was suffering from a wasting
illness, he was cured by his father Lugh, but the greatest divine
influence on the hero was from the battle-furies, the Morrigán and
the Badbh, both of whom sometimes appeared in triplicate, could
change shape at will and were seen on the battlefield in the form of
carrion crows picking over the dead. The most striking encounter
between Cú Chulainn and these fearsome goddesses was during the
conflict over the two great bulls of Ulster and Connacht.

The hero was approached by a young noblewoman, who told
him that she loved him, admired him for his great deeds, and had
brought him gifts of treasure and cattle. Cú Chulainn's churlish
reply was that he could not be bothered with sex at the moment; he
had far more important things on his mind. His rudeness revealed
the girl's true identity as the Morrigán: she threatened to attack him

at a river-ford first as an eel, then as a grey she-wolf and finally as a hornless red heifer. His own counter-threats caused her to leave him, for the time being.

The hero's death was predicted by the appearance of the 'Washer at the Ford', a guise of the Morrigán, who washed the armour of those about to be slain. When he mounted his chariot, all his weapons fell at his feet, as though consciously abandoning him (or perhaps mourning for him). Cú Chulainn suffered mortal injuries on the battlefield, killed as only a hero could be, with a weapon made by a god, a spear forged by the smith-god Vulcan. Knowing that he was about to die, he bound himself to a stake so that he

Lifesize bronze sculpture of the dying Cú Chulainn, tied to a tree to stop him falling, the Badbh as battle-crow on his shoulder. By Oliver Shepherd, 1916, for the main Post Office, Dublin.

would die upright, facing the enemy: the hero-light dimmed round his head and, as the life went out of him, the Morrigán, also known as the Badbh, perched on his shoulder in the form of a crow, to signal to his enemies that he was dead and safe to approach.

• PRYDERI AND THE WELSH HEROIC TRADITION •

The boy was brought up at the court until he was a year old. And before he was a year old he was walking strongly, and was sturdier than a well-developed and well-grown three-year-old boy. The boy was reared a second year, and he was as sturdy as a six-year-old. And before the end of the fourth year he was bargaining with the stableboys to be allowed to water the horses.
FROM THE FIRST BRANCH OF THE *MABINOGI*

To be a Celtic hero, you needed a special childhood, like Cú Chulainn's. This was certainly true of Pryderi, the son of Pwyll, lord of Llys Arberth, and his wife Rhiannon, herself a supernatural creature, a horse-goddess. We have already heard (see pp. 81–83) how when their son was born he disappeared and his mother was severely punished. But what became of the baby stolen from Rhiannon's side while she slept?

The location of the tale shifts from Llys Arberth to Gwent-Iscoed, the court of its lord Teyrnon Twryf Liant. His household had been blighted for years by a strange event that took place every May-eve: at that time his prize mare always gave birth to a superb foal, which disappeared no sooner than it was born. On the very night that Rhiannon and Pwyll's baby boy disappeared, Teyrnon decided to stay up all night and keep watch in his stable to try and get to the bottom of the mystery.

As soon as his mare had birthed her foal, a huge claw appeared at the window and snatched up the colt, dragging it through the aperture. Teyrnon immediately struck out, severed the clawed hand and

Hidden Shamans

The tales where Cú Chulainn takes centre stage provide subtle clues as to possible origins deep in the pre-medieval past. They are shot through with imagery that hints at an underlying tradition of shamanism. The Ulster champion experienced a shamanic out-of-body state when in berserk, 'warp-spasm' mode. His close links with dogs and horses suggest that these beasts were spirit-helpers that belonged to a shaman and assisted in liaising between earth- and spirit-forces.

The Morrigán was a shape-shifter, a classic sign of the shaman. The episode in the *Táin Bó Cuailnge* where the Morrigán exercised her power to shape-shift at a ford is also redolent with shamanism. In many shamanistic traditions, shallow water is associated with shamanic ritual because here the membrane between the earthly and spiritual worlds is thought to be at its thinnest.

Bronze horse from Neuvy-en-Sullias, France.

Iron age gold coin minted by the Redones of Brittany, depicting a naked horsewoman
brandishing a spear and shield.

retrieved the foal. As he did so, he heard an otherworldly scream
and the sound of a commotion outside. He rushed out to see what
was going on but saw nothing in the darkness. On returning to the
stable, there was a fine baby boy lying on the threshold, wrapped in
a shawl of brocaded silk, an indication of his noble birth.

Terynon and his wife decided to keep the child and raise him
as their own, naming him Gwri Golden Hair because of his bright
blond head. They soon began to notice that the little boy far out-
stripped others of his age and, at a year old, was bigger than a child
three times his age. Now the myth-spinner cleverly began to close
the circle of symbolism enclosing the tale. The audience had probably already guessed that this child was none other than Rhiannon
and Pwyll's missing son, but before the child's true identity was
revealed, the storyteller set the scene for the dénouement.

When Gwri was four years old, Terynon's wife suggested that
their colt should be broken in and given to the child. This provided a
neat anticipatory connection between Rhiannon's horse-affiliation
and that of her son. The mythic circle was finally closed when news
of Pwyll's missing son arrived at Gwent-Iscoed; Teyrnon realized
how like Pwyll their foster-son was, and he returned him to Llys

Arberth, amid great rejoicing at the court of his parents. Rhiannon was released from her penance, and she renamed the boy Pryderi, a word for 'care' or 'worry'.

As in the story of Cú Chulainn, the essential characteristics of a supernatural hero were woven into the narrative of Pryderi. Somehow, Rhiannon escaped being executed, despite the double crime – infanticide and cannibalism – of which she stood accused. The baby vanished in an inexplicable fashion and was found far away, on a threshold, a significant location that traditionally symbolized the betwixt-and-between spaces where earthly and spiritual domains could meet. Added to the mix was Pryderi's affinity with horses and, in particular, with a male foal born at the same time as himself and with which he was exchanged by some enchantment. The crowning badge of Pryderi's status as a hero was, of course, his precocity and, like his Ulster counterpart, he went on to become the most beautiful and accomplished of men.

The goddess Epona in her usual pose, mounted and bearing fruit. The divine horsewoman may have inspired the myth of Rhiannon.

· 6 ·

ENCHANTING ANIMALS AND EDGY BEINGS

*'Eagle of Gwernabwy, we have come to you – Arthur's
messengers – to ask if you know anything of Mabon, son
of Modron who was taken when three nights old from
his mother?'*
*The Eagle said, 'I came here a long time ago, and when
I first came here I had a rock, and from its top I would
peck at the stars every evening.'*
FROM 'CULHWCH AND OLWEN'

The foundation stone of Celtic mythologies was the perception that spirits lurked in every corner of the landscape. The relationship between people and their perceived spirit-world could be an uneasy one, full of risk and instability. The boundaries between these domains could shift and become permeable, allowing mutual encroachment. Fundamental to the persistent presence of shape-shifting beings and magical animals seems to have been the underlying principle that the material world inhabited by people was inherently unstable, rather like earthquake zones on shifting tectonic plates. The ability of divinities to interfere with human lives was paramount in the Celtic myths.

Although their presence was never spelled out in the stories, there are clues to the shamanic status of many individuals who had the ability to move between worlds, and the agency for so doing was often the capacity to take on the form of animals. The 'normal' scheme of things was capable of being overturned: animals and humans could exchange physical forms; gods could appear to people in the shape of fellow humans, beasts or monsters; and goddesses might shift between the forms of youthful maiden, mature matron and old crone.

Transgressors might be transformed into animals as punishment but, conversely, beasts were sometimes endowed with human skills, such as speech, and some possessed prophetic powers. Some animals – particularly certain dogs, horses and cattle – were clearly sent from the Otherworld. The clues to their origins lay in their appearance: they were dazzling white, red or white with red ears. The medieval storyteller would use such devices as the colour of animals to convey notions of magic and enchantment to the audience and, in their turn, those listening to the tales would be familiar with these coded messages and their meaning.

● MATH'S CURSE ●

Then he took his magic wand, and struck Gilfaethwy so that
he changed into a good-sized hind, and he caught Gwydion
quickly – he could not escape although he wanted to – and
struck him with the same magic wand so that he changed
into a stag.
'Since you are in league with each other, I will make you live
together and mate with each other.'
FROM THE FOURTH BRANCH OF THE *MABINOGI*

In the Irish myths, shape-changing, between human and animal form, was often a voluntary transition. For instance, the battle goddesses – the Morrígán and the Badbh – turned at will from woman to carrion crow and back again. In the Welsh mythic tradition, however, shape-shifting was frequently inflicted as a punishment for misconduct. And so it was for the nephews of King Math of Gwynedd. When Gwydion and Gilfaethwy conspired to rob Math's foot-holder, Goewin, of her virginity (see pp. 84–86), they struck at the very roots of Math's power. So it is no surprise that he wreaked swift and horrific vengeance upon the brothers, denying them their humanity and even their gender.

He turned them into three different pairs of wild animals for each of three years. The first year Gilfaethwy became a hind and his brother a stag; at the end of the year, they appeared at Math's court with their fawn. The next year, their genders were exchanged: Gwydion became a wild sow and Gilfaethwy a wild boar, and at the end of the year, the couple presented themselves at the court with their piglet. The following year, the errant brothers were turned into wolves, and produced a wolf-cub.

At the end of the third year, Math lifted the enchantment, but their offspring, although of human shape, each retained the ability to shape-shift to their animal form. The children were baptized and named after their animal forms: Hyddwn (stag), Hychdwn (pig) and Bleiddwn (wolf). A sign of their magical nature was demonstrated by their precocity. Like the heroes Cú Chulainn and Pryderi, they were far too well grown for their mortal age, a sign that they were touched by the numinous hand of Math, the magician.

• THE SALMON OF WISDOM •

Three times Cúchulainn tried to cross the bridge but his best
efforts failed, and the men jeered him. Then he went into his
warp-spasm. He stepped to the head of the bridge and gave his
hero's salmon-leap onto the middle.
FROM THE *TÁIN BÓ CUAILNGE*

Connections between the Welsh and Irish mythic traditions are nowhere more explicit than in the common story of the magical salmon that possessed the gifts of knowledge, wisdom and prophecy, far in excess of any human capacity. Why this creature should have been woven into the rich tapestry of legends about people, beasts and links with the spirits is not immediately evident. But it is likely that observation of the salmon's complex life-history, its travels through great distances, involving considerable physical effort, in both fresh and salt water, its unerring instinct to return to its home waters to breed, and its seeming capacity to fly up water-falls, may all have led to the salmon's imagined supernatural and super-intellectual qualities.

The wise salmon-myth is contained within the Fenian Cycle, whose eponymous hero was Finn. The story is redolent with sha-manism, for the young boy Finn acquired his gifts through the agency of the bard Finnegas (note the shared name-root) who lived on the banks of the river Boyne, an enchanted watery space, the personification of the goddess Boann, and a gateway to the spirit-world. At the moment of encounter between Finn and Finnegas, the latter was fishing for the renowned Salmon of Wisdom in a pool, an activity upon which he had been engaged in vain for seven years. The Salmon had received its gifts from its consumption of nuts pro-duced by nine magical hazel trees growing on the seabed.

As Finn approached him, Finnegas caught the fish and passed it to the boy with instructions to cook it over a fire. While doing so, the young hero accidentally touched the searing hot flesh of the fish with his thumb and instinctively put it in his mouth to ease the pain. Instantly, he was endowed with all the wisdom and knowledge the salmon possessed, and became a great seer. Indeed, Finn's act gave rise to the Irish idea of the 'seer's thumb', and the belief that the thumb might hold particular spiritual potency. This tale resonates with the Welsh story 'Ceridwen's Cauldron' (see p. 28) in which the young Gwion, tending a cauldron, accidentally acquired knowl-edge from being splashed on the hand by its contents, intended for Ceridwen's ill-favoured son Afagddu.

A Welsh version of the Salmon of Wisdom is contained in the tale of 'Culhwch and Olwen'. In his quest to find the divine hunter Mabon, son of Modron (their names mean 'Young Son' and 'Mother') to secure his help finding Olwen, Culhwch consulted a series of enchanted beasts that had the capacity to communicate with humans and, in particular, with one of Arthur's men Gwrhyr

'Interpreter of Tongues'. One of these talking animals was the Salmon of Llyn Llyw, one of the oldest (and therefore wisest) creatures on earth.

Gwrhyr learned of the Salmon's existence through another speaking beast, the Eagle of Gwernabwy, which had tried to catch the fish but, instead, had been drawn deep into the water. The bird and the fish had made peace and the Eagle thought that the Salmon might be able to help Gwrhyr and his fellow knight Cei to find Mabon. The bird duly summoned up the Salmon and it agreed to help. It ushered the two men onto its vast shoulders and took them to find Mabon where he was languishing in prison. He was eventually freed by Arthur's warriors and joined in Culhwch's quest for Olwen.

Iron Age granite image with outsize and upraised thumbs, from Lanneunoc, Brittany.

The Seer's Thumb

Young Finn's scorched thumb inadvertently gave him all the Salmon of Wisdom's knowledge. The so-called 'seer's thumb' may in fact belong to a stratum of Celtic tradition that pre-dates the early medieval collections of tales. For in late Iron Age Gaul, divine images were sometimes depicted with extra-large, upraised thumbs. Some of the wild mounted goddesses on Breton coins depict female charioteers (perhaps early forebears of Medbh, see pp. 140–41) holding the reins with giant thumbs erect. A granite statue from Lanneunoc, also in Brittany, depicts a headless torso, virtually without detail except for a pair of very large hands with prominent and upraised thumbs. One of the late Iron Age bog-bodies from Lindow Moss in Cheshire had extra thumbs. Is it possible he was perceived as a seer?

Bronze figurine of a Romano-British war-god grasping a ram-horned snake in each hand.

• MIXED-UP BODIES: •
THE ARCHAEOLOGY OF SHAPE-SHIFTING

I'll come in the shape of a grey she-wolf, to stampede the beasts into the ford against you.
I'll come before you in the shape of a hornless red heifer and lead the cattle-herd to trample you in the waters, by ford and pool, and you won't know me.

FROM AN ENCOUNTER BETWEEN CÚ CHULAINN AND
THE MORRIGÁN, IN THE *TÁIN BÓ CUAILNGE*

The permeability and blurring of edges between humans and animals so explicit in the mythology is paralleled in the iconographic record of the Western European Iron Age and the Roman provincial period. Imagery is shot through with ambiguities of form: bulls or boars might be depicted with three horns, horses with human faces and snakes with ram's horns. Half-human creatures are common in

One of the inner plates of the Iron Age silver cauldron from Gundestrup, Denmark, depicting an antlered god holding a ram-horned snake.

the iconographic repertoire. The most persistent hybrids are man/ stag images, most strikingly featured on the Gundestrup Cauldron, where an antlered man sits surrounded by animals, including a stag with identical antlers that stands close beside him, as though in the act of morphing from one state to the other.

Gender-twisting is also involved in antlered figures, for some Gallic bronze figurines depict women with many-branched antlers sprouting from their heads. We do not have a name for this antlered human, but we do have one clue, from an image on a carved stone column from Paris, set up in honour of Jupiter in AD 26. Among a plethora of Classical and native Gallic religious iconography on this monument appears a bearded, antlered head, a torc or neck-ring hanging from each antler. Above is a worn inscription 'Cernunno' ('to the horned one').

The mixing-up of bodies is also recorded in Iron Age human remains. Some burial deposits contain a blend of human and animal body-parts as if to exhibit perceptions of the porosity of boundaries between them. Both the osteological and iconograph- ical records appear to present a way of thinking about the world

Cat-people

Thus was Cairbre the cruel
who seized Ireland south and north:
two cat's ears on his fair head
a cat's fur through his ears.

FROM A MEDIEVAL IRISH POEM BY EOCHAID UA FLOINN

This poem is preserved in a 12th-century text. Its central character was a warlord called Cairbre the Cruel. The animal-features of this handsome man are probably a reference to the bestial and merciless nature of a cruel conqueror, but the specific allusion to cats may refer, too, to his cunning and stealth. However, the poet may also have been tapping into an ancient shamanistic tradition in which holy men and women donned animal costume during ceremonies in order to attain affinity with the spirits. Images of men with cats' ears are found in Roman Britain: clay roofing-tiles from Caerleon in south Wales depict cat-eared human heads; and a bearded stone head with pointed ears has been recorded from Doncaster in Yorkshire.

Clay antefix (roofing-tile) depicting a human head with cats' ears, from the Roman legionary fortress at Caerleon, South Wales.

Stone carving of a human head wearing antlers, with torcs hanging from them.
From a monument in Paris dedicated to Jupiter in AD 26 by a guild of Seine boatmen.

in which thresholds were crossed and borders transgressed in
order – perhaps – to demonstrate perceptions of fluidity and the
ability of humans and beasts to exchange forms in both directions.
It is entirely possible that the presence of shape-shifting in Celtic
mythology reflects a much earlier, possibly shamanic, tradition that
recognized the importance of animals as conduits between worlds
and the necessity for humans to assume animal-bodies for spiritual
communication.

• RAVEN VOICES: THE IRISH BATTLE-HAGS •

A strong mythic tradition in the Ulster Cycle is the association of
goddesses with warfare. They did not themselves take part in the
fighting but they interfered, causing tension between the opposing
forces, encouraging bloodshed and, more sinisterly, they could be
seen picking over the corpses of the slain on the battlefield. These
dark deities were concerned above all with death, but they were

also promiscuous, sexually insatiable and intent on seducing young heroes such as Cú Chulainn, as we have seen (pp. 110–12).

The two principal battle-furies were the Badbh and the Morrigán and, to a degree, their identities merged. Each had the capacity for multi-layered shape-shifting: from young maiden to old crone, from one to three, and from woman to raven or carrion-crow. Prophetesses of untimely and violent death, they could also blur visual gender-boundaries: appearing as an ancient, bearded hag. The association between crows/ ravens and the dead is an obvious one: the birds are shiny black and feed on carrion, whether animal or human. Such birds must have been frequent and primary visitors to scenes of mass slaughter and their hunched bodies, picking off bits of meat from dead warriors, lent them the appearance of ancient crones. The blurring of the boundary between bird and woman was enhanced by the croaking but human-like 'voice' of the raven, together with its ability to mimic human speech.

A curious archaeological phenomenon from the late Iron Age of southern Britain is the recurrent ritual deposition of raven-bones. It has long been recognized that people occupying hillforts in Wessex dug deep grain silos to store seed-corn over the winter but that, after secular use, they were methodically cleaned out and filled with human and animal remains. This was not rubbish, but carefully structured offerings of whole or partial bodies of people and animals. The latter belonged almost exclusively to domestic species, the exception being the persistent presence of ravens, in far greater numbers than reflected in the living population.

Such a divergence from the usual tradition of depositing horses, dogs and sheep requires explanation. Perhaps, as in the later mythologies, these birds were symbols of death and warfare. But it has been suggested that the remains of ravens were present because their feathers were used to adorn the headdresses of priests or shamans on ceremonial occasions. Dressing up in animal-costumes, including antlers and feathers, may have played an important part

Shamanic Bird-Men of Ireland

The birds left their feather hoods, then, and turned on Conaire with spears and swords; one bird protected him, however, saying, 'I am Nemglan, king of your father's bird-troop.'

FROM 'DA DERGA'S HOSTEL'

Two mythic tales contain powerful images of shape-shifting seers who donned the 'form' of birds in order for their souls to fly between the layers of the cosmos and operate as two-spirit beings. 'The Siege of Druim Damghaire' chronicles the contest between King Cormac of Ulster and Mog Ruith, a blind prophet, both of whom claimed to possess magical powers superior to the other's. In order to tap into the spirit world and thus win the contest, Mog Ruith donned a bull-hide cloak and a headdress made of speckled birds' feathers. The dappled colour is significant, for the dual colouring evoked Mog Ruith's liminal status as belonging both to the material and the spiritual world.

Because of his bird-form, the seer was able to fly and to summon up spiritual support against Cormac's magic. The prophet's physical blindness is also key to understanding his status as a seer, for many prophets in antiquity were afflicted in this way, resulting in the in 'shape-shifting' rituals. Could it be that here lay the roots of later Celtic legends of raven-women such as the Badbh?

Iconography from Iron Age and Roman Europe frequently depicts 'bird-people': humans dressed up as birds or – perhaps – realizations of spirits in half-avian form. They are persistent themes in Late Bronze Age rock-art from Sweden and on Iron Age petroglyphs at Camonica Valley in northern Italy. One Swedish panel, from Kallsängen in Bohuslän, is carved with images of human bodies that have beaked heads and wings; one of them deviates even

Opposite: Iron Age rock-carving of a bird-man, from Camonica Valley, Italy. The shamanic practice of wearing feathered wings dates back over 5000 years.

---

sharpening of their inner visionary powers: Tiresias of Greek mythology and the Israelite Ahijah of the Old Testament were both blind. In certain modern shamanistic communities – among the Sora of India for instance – shamanic seers cover their faces when entering trance-state, attaining thought-vision and the ability to liaise with the spirits.

A bird-man called Nemglan was closely associated with the mythical Irish ruler Conaire Mór, whose life is described in the story 'Da Derga's Hostel'. The entire tale is shot through with allusions to enchantment, magic and the porous boundaries between the worlds of people and the gods. Like the Ulster hero Cú Chulainn, Conaire Mor was bound by a *geis* or prohibition: he was not allowed to hunt or kill any bird. This injunction was laid down by his father at the time he was conceived. When he was about to assume the kingship, Conaire was instructed by Nemglan, who laid a series of *gessa* upon the new king and reinforced the ban on inflicting injury upon birds. On one occasion, Conaire disobeyed his bird-*geis* and the flock of birds he tried to kill shed all their feathers and attacked him. Chief of the bird-troop was Nemglan, a shape-shifter, who tried to protect Conaire from the rest of the flock. Like Mog Ruith, Nemglan was a shaman, a two-spirit being, able to cross the threshold between people, animals and the spirit world.

Stone relief of a divine forester, with a hound, club, an open bag of fruit and on each shoulder a raven, from Moux, Burgundy.

more as it portrays a double-headed (Janus-type) figure that looks both ways.

Though the Scandinavian material seems to depict 'genuine' half-human creatures, the Camonican bird-people are less ambiguous images and clearly depicts men or women dressed in bird-costume. In Roman Gaul, bird-men are not presented as merged human and bird forms, but as bird-guardians. A sculpture from Moux in Burgundy is that of a protector of the woodland: he carries oak-apples, a stave and billhook, and is accompanied by a hound and two large-beaked, raven-like birds that perch on his shoulder and turn to gaze intimately into his face, perhaps whispering in his ears.

• LABOURS OF LOVE: CULHWCH AND OLWEN •

Then Culhwch's father said to him, 'Son, why are you blushing?
What's the matter?'
'My stepmother has sworn that I may never have a wife until
I get Olwen daughter of Ysbaddaden Bencawr.'
'It is easy for you to get that, son,' said his father to him. 'Arthur
is your cousin. Go to Arthur to have your hair trimmed, and
ask him for that as your gift.'
FROM 'CULHWCH AND OLWEN'

Another common animal in the Welsh tales is the pig. We have seen its importance as a food at feasts, and the high esteem in which it was held as bravest and most fearsome of animals (see p. 102). The story most redolent with pig-symbolism is 'Culhwch and Olwen'. The eponymous hero's name means 'pig-run'. Culhwch was of high birth, being Arthur's cousin. The association with pigs is introduced at the beginning of the story, and the hero's pig-connection began even before he was born. When pregnant with him, Culhwch's mother Goleuddydd developed an overwhelming antipathy to these creatures. One day, as she accidentally encountered a herd of swine, her fright brought on her premature labour and, as soon as the baby was born, she abandoned him. He was discovered by the swineherd and given his 'pig-run' name because that was where he was found.

Culhwch's link with pigs stayed with him. He grew up and fell in love with Olwen, daughter of a giant named Ysbaddaden. Olwen's father made all sorts of objections to the match and imposed upon her suitor a series of Herculean tasks or labours that were virtually impossible to achieve. The very fact that Culhwch managed to carry out the tasks provides clues as to his superhuman heroic status. The core of the Culhwch and Olwen myth was the most insuperable task of all: Ysbaddaden demanded the scissors, razor and comb from between the ears of Twrch Trwyth, an enormous supernatural boar, once a human king.

Because of his association with pigs since birth, it is appropriate that Culhwch should be pitted against such an enemy as the Twrch – it is as though they were bound together in opposition: good against evil, blessed against cursed. The very description of the Twrch immediately let listeners know that he came from the Otherworld, not only because of his great size but on account of his bristles that glistened like shining silver wings. Culhwch enlisted the help of King Arthur in this seemingly impossible quest, for the Twrch was a formidable opponent, but the good finally prevailed over the evil; the grooming equipment was taken from between the beast's ears and the magical boar driven into the sea. Culhwch used the razor, shears and comb on Ysbaddaden's beard and Olwen was won. Culhwch and Olwen were married and lived happily and monogamously until death claimed them.

• AN ENCHANTMENT OF BULLS •

This was the Brown Bull of Cuailnge –
dark brown dire haughty with young health
horrific overwhelming ferocious
full of craft
furious fiery flanks narrow
brave brutal thick breasted
curly browed head cocked high
growling and eyes glaring
tough maned neck thick and strong....
FROM THE *TÁIN BÓ CUAILNGE*

Cattle were central to early medieval Irish prosperity: they were units of wealth and a ruler's status was measured by the number and splendour of his herds. The importance of cattle in Irish society is shown to great effect in the *Táin Bó Cuailnge*, whose central focus is two enormous and enchanted bulls. Early on in the tale, it is revealed that these bulls were no ordinary beasts. The Brown, or Donn, was so big that fifty boys could dance on his back. The Finnbennach (White-Horned Bull) of Connacht had a red body, a white head and white feet; these colours indicative of its emanation from the Otherworld. Both bulls had begun their lives as human swineherds, but had been transformed into animals who retained their capacity for human reasoning and language. Their struggle to the death, each representing their native provinces of Ulster and Connacht, epitomizes their role as personifications of their lands, their fertility and prosperity.

Gallo-British iconography of the late pre-Roman Iron Age and the Roman period *may* contain glimpses of traditions from which sprang the idea of enchanted cattle. The Gundestrup Cauldron is steeped in the imagery of bull-sacrifice. These animals were clearly supernatural creatures, for they are depicted on the cauldron as being much bigger than life-size, in contrast with their diminutive human killers.

The *Tarbhfess*

The bull-symbolism on the Gundestrup Cauldron calls to mind a curious mythic Irish ritual, that of the *Tarbhfhess* or 'bull-sleep'. The legend was particularly associated with the royal site of Tara, and connected with choosing the right king of Ireland. A bull was slaughtered, butchered and cooked; a specially chosen individual then consumed the flesh and broth. After his meal, he lay down to sleep, while four Druids chanted over him until they received a vision in which the identity of the next rightful king was revealed to them.

An Ancient Gaulish Bull-myth

In AD 26, a guild of boatmen who sailed the river Seine dedicated a great stone pillar to Jupiter in Paris. The monument was inscribed with the names of several deities, each with its accompanying carved image. Some of the gods invoked were Roman, but others belonged to a local pantheon. One of the panels bears the inscription 'Tarvos Trigaranus', the 'Bull with Three Cranes'. The image beneath is of a huge bull, standing in front of a willow tree. Two egrets or cranes perch on his back, a third on his head. Egrets and willows both like water, so that may explain the association between the birds and the tree. These birds also enjoy a symbiotic relationship with cattle in that they feed on parasites on their hides.

Stone carving of Tarvos Trigaranus, the bull with three cranes, from a monument dedicated by a Parisian boatmen's guild in AD 26.

But certain features are suggestive of a lost mythic narrative, and this is reinforced by the presence of a virtually identical image far away to the east at Trier on the river Moselle. On both monuments, the scene of the bull and three egrets is associated with the image of a woodman pruning a willow. On the Paris stone, the woodman bears the name Esus. In his epic poem *The Pharsalia* (its theme the great civil war between Pompey and Julius Caesar), the Roman poet Lucan mentions three fearsome Gallic gods: Taranis, Teutates and Esus. It is almost certain that Lucan was speaking of the same 'Esus' that is recorded on the monument from Paris.

The Capel Garmon Fire-dog

Some time during the late 1st or early 2nd century AD, someone made a journey to a remote marsh in the far northwest of Wales, a place today known as Capel Garmon (Carmon's Chapel). They carried with them a large, heavy and highly ornate piece of iron hearth-furniture, ornamented with bulls' heads, which was probably used in spit-roasting meat or simply as a fender to guard the cooking-fire. Many such 'fire-dogs' have been found in Britain and Gaul, but this one is special both because it is so decorative and so evocative of consummate blacksmithing skill and because it appears to have been 'sacrificed'.

A horizontal cross-piece connects two uprights, each of which terminates in the head of a horned beast. But the two heads are not depictions of ordinary bulls – instead they are 'baroque' creatures, for they each have elaborate manes, like those of dressage horses, formed of linked iron balls. Close scrutiny of the Capel Garmon piece reveals that each animal head was unique, indicative of the intent to produce images of two individual beasts, with different faces. The description of the bulls in the *Táin Bó Cuailnge* chimes with the Capel Garmon fire-dog, for these enchanted creatures, too, had manes and they too were spirit-creatures, conjured from the Otherworld.

Whether or not the Capel Garmon fire-dog was ever used is not certain. But it had a life and a death, for its biography drew to a close when it was deliberately placed in a bog, with a large stone placed on top of each bull's head, in the manner of ancient human bog-burials. The fire-dog was a highly valued and special object. A modern Welsh blacksmith who has attempted to replicate the object estimates that it took as long as three years of a metal-worker's life to produce. Given that these fire-dogs were meant to be used in pairs, its value, in terms of human resources, must have been staggering. It may have had as much, if not more, 'currency' as a sacrifice as a living human did. The weird nature of the bulls, with their horses' manes, only made them more fantastic evocations of spirit-animals.

Late Iron Age iron fire-dog decorated with maned bulls heads, from Capel Garmon, north Wales.

• THE OWL AND THE EAGLE: •
A WELSH MYTH OF NIGHT AND DAY

The Fourth Branch of the *Mabinogi* is full of shape-shifting. Math's punishment-curse when he transformed Gwydion and Gilfaethwy, considered earlier in this chapter, is not the only episode where boundaries between humans and animals were crossed. The kernel of this same tale concerns a fatal love-triangle, between a beautiful young girl, Blodeuwedd, her husband Lleu Llaw Gyffes and a third man, Gronw.

To put the story into context, it is necessary for a brief recap on the background to Lleu's predicament. After the rape of Goewin, Arianrhod came forward as a candidate to be Math's foot-holder, but she failed the virginity test by giving birth to twins. It is around the second-born child that the main tale is woven. In her shame, Arianrhod repudiated this second son, Lleu, and put upon him three curses, meant to prevent him from taking his place in society.

Gwydion and his uncle Math pooled their magical resources to find a way past Arianrhod's injunction and contrive a way of obtaining Lleu a wife. They managed this by conjuring a woman from flowers called Blodeuwedd. But she took a lover, Gronw, and together they plotted how to murder her husband. Lleu's own magical nature was now revealed, for, alongside the negative prohibitions laid upon him by his mother, were another set, this time designed to protect him. He could not be killed either inside or outside a house, neither on water nor on land, neither naked nor clad.

Furthermore, Lleu could only be wounded by a spear made during the times when smithing was not permitted. All these conditions involve edges and boundaries, and were signs that Lleu himself was deeply involved with forces from the Otherworld. By fiendish cunning, Blodeuwedd tricked the credulous Lleu into revealing the secret formula by which his death-injunctions could be overcome, and he confessed to her:

By making a bath for me on a river bank, and making a vaulted frame over the tub, and thatching it well and snugly too thereafter, and bringing a he-goat,' said he, 'and setting it beside the tub, and myself placing one foot of the back of the he-goat and the other on the edge of the tub. Whoever should smite me so, he would bring about my death.'

FROM THE FOURTH BRANCH OF THE *MABINOGI*

Meanwhile, Gronw had secretly laboured to make the fatal spear, tipping it with poison, and, when he had done so, Blodeuwedd persuaded Lleu to adopt the position he had described to her; Gronw leapt out from hiding and delivered his rival a mortal injury.

But instead of falling down dead, Lleu gave a huge scream and flew away in the form of an eagle. Gwydion discovered what had happened and he cursed Blodeuwedd, turning her into an owl condemned to hunt at night and shunned by all other birds because

Bronze figurine of an eagle, from the Romano-British temple at Woodeaton, Oxfordshire.

of her shame. He also found Lleu, perched in an oak-tree, and restored him to human form. The wronged husband slew Gronw and assumed the lordship of Gwynedd.

The striking thing about this story is that it presents a hidden myth of good and evil. Because Blodeuwedd was not mortal, she was fundamentally flawed, untrustworthy and ultimately too dangerous to be among humans. Lleu's shape-change – as well as his name 'Bright One' and his mother's name Arianrhod 'Silver Wheel' – reveals that he was a sky-god, and his refuge in an oak reinforces that connection. In Classical mythology, both the eagle and the oak were associated with the Roman celestial god Jupiter. But the Welsh tale is coloured with Christian moral dogma. Magical practices, such as conjuring women from flowers, were to be condemned. Right would ultimately prevail, and the light would shine through and conquer the dark side.

Devils: From Myth to Tarot

Celtic myth is infused with portraits of evil women with unnatural appearance, but what of devils? In modern occultism, as presented on tarot-cards, the Devil is portrayed as a seated half-human creature, horned, goat-headed, cloven-hoofed being, with a beard and female breasts. In medieval Europe, the Devil was portrayed with horns and often resembled the much earlier iconography of the antlered 'Cernunnos'. There is no hint at a dark side in the Celtic presentation of Cernunnos himself, but his human/beast ambiguity fed into early Christian notions of bestiality, pagan chaos and contradictions of the notion that humans has been fashioned in the image of God.

7

DANGEROUS LIAISONS:
MONSTROUS REGIMENTS OF WOMEN

*A whole troop of foreigners would not be able to withstand a
single Gaul if he called his wife to his assistance, who is usually
very strong and with blue eyes; especially when, swelling her
neck, gnashing her teeth, and brandishing her sallow arms of
enormous size, she begins to strike blows mingled with kicks,
if they were so many missiles sent from the string of a catapult.*
AMMIANUS MARCELLINUS, *HISTORIES* XV.12

In his powerful tragedy *The Bacchae*, the Athenian dramatist
Euripides played out his feelings of turbulence and despair after
enduring more than 20 years of bloody civil war between Sparta
and his native city-state. The play was written in 407 BC, after the
playwright had fled from Athens to the relative peace and calm
of Macedon. The central theme of the drama is the two opposing
aspects of human (more specifically, man's) nature, the civilized and
the savage, and the tensions of *nomos* (order) and *physis* (nature).

The relevance of Euripides' tragedy to Celtic myths lies in the
way in which women are presented. *The Bacchae* places women,
animals and the untamed natural world on the wild side of the
divide, in fundamental opposition to the ordered civilized world
of men, order and the built environment (cities). Women were
weak and thus subject to the excesses of the wild and, while under
the intoxicating influence of the god Dionysus, they were capable
of sexual mayhem, and of dreadful acts of violence, including the
killing, dismemberment and consumption of humans.

The treatment of many prominent women in the Welsh and
– particularly – the Irish mythic texts appears to show female characters in a similarly unflattering (and decidedly unfeminist) light.

Such portrayals are at least partly due to their chroniclers, Christian clerics for whom proper women had no public presence and whose virginity was to be jealously guarded. And so the Ulster Cycle treats Queen Medbh of Connacht as a woman of uncontrolled sexual and military appetites, who was frequently ridiculed by her narrators. Even her death was ignominious: she was killed by a slingshot made from a ball of hard cheese. Stories about other Irish female 'heroes',

---

Witches in Myth and Shakespeare

The three hideous witches who both foretell and bring about Macbeth's destruction in Shakespeare's powerful tragedy bear a strong resemblance to the Badbh and the Morrigán of Irish myth. Like them, Macbeth's witches are old, amoral, skilled in prophecy and sexually ambiguous: Banquo says

'You should be women
and yet your beards forbid me to interpret
that you are so.'

Shakespeare wrote The Scottish Play in the time of King James I's anti-witch fervour, an attitude fuelled by the conspiracy of Scottish witches to murder him uncovered in 1591. Shakespeare deliberately presented the witches as beyond all human decency: vengeful, destructive and purveyors of horrific rituals. In the witch-trials of the time, it was declared that victims were put under spells because of a refusal to give a witch hospitality. This is exactly how the Irish king Conaire Mor was destroyed by the Badbh in the tale of 'Da Derga's Hostel'. Like the Ulster hero Cú Chulainn, Conaire Mor was doomed by a double *geis*: as well as the bird-*geis* described above (p. 127), he was forbidden to be alone with a woman after sunset, but bound also by the universal laws of hospitality, which forced him to entertain her. Inevitably, Conaire Mór's double-bind brought about his downfall. Directed by the Badbh, his enemies struck off his head. But Conaire's strange bond with the Otherworld is further shown in this story, for his severed head spoke to his comrade-in-arms Mac Cécht, who avenged the king's death.

Inner plate from the Gundestrup cauldron, Denmark. It depicts the head and shoulders of a woman, flanked by two wheels.

such as Deirdre of the Sorrows (see pp. 73–74), emphasize the downfall of men beguiled by their beauty. Their Welsh counterparts were not so harshly treated in the literature, but they were for the most part colourless, important only as catalysts for male action. Rhiannon and Blodeuwedd stand out as exceptions but, even so, their fortunes were dictated by men.

• MILITARY WIVES: MEDBH AND MACHA •

Medbh turned back again from the north after spending a
fortnight harassing the province. She had attacked Finn-mór,
wife of Celtchar mac Uthidir, and taken fifty women from her
at the capture of Dún Sobairche in the territory of Dál Riada.
FROM THE *TÁIN BÓ CUAILNGE*

Medbh features strongly in the Ulster Cycle. In the cataclysmic conflict between the two Irish provinces of Ulster and Connacht, as recorded in the *Táin Bó Cuailnge*, it was her jealousy of the Great

Brown Bull of Ulster that caused her to instigate the great war that would end in a hollow victory. Medbh was the elected ruler of Connacht. Her consort, Ailill, played a minimal role: all the power was hers. She was violent, bloodthirsty, cunning and promiscuous and, in possessing these 'qualities', she went against everything considered appropriate for medieval Christian women. The literature that describes her activities screams disapproval from its pages, and the prediction 'it'll all end in tears' is the constantly whispered message. And so it did.

Medbh's very name betrays her character, for it means 'She who Intoxicates'. According to the mythic texts, she ruled Connacht from the royal centres of Tara and Cruachain. She was almost certainly a deity rather than an earthly queen, but was 'euhemerized' (presented as a person rather than a divinity) in the literature. In essence, Medbh was a goddess of sovereignty, one of several Irish divine females who conferred kingship upon mortal rulers. She, like her sisters, was concerned with three main things: sexuality (which gave Ireland its fertility), war (which defended it) and territory (which safeguarded its people).

The Christian moral principles held by the monastic redactor (writer of tales) shows through in Medbh's excesses. Everything about her was extreme, immoderate and – to Christian eyes – unseemly. She was a drunkard, she was a destroyer, she adored sex and was able to unman the most virile hero by the ferocious speed with which she drove round the battlefield in her chariot. It is easy to see a close parallel between Medbh and Euripides's maenads in *The Bacchae*. She and her opponent, the Ulster king Conchobar, were two of a kind, for he was cruel and treacherous, and the two were evenly matched. Medbh's divine credentials show through her apparent human form: like many gods and shamans, she possessed animal spirit-helpers, in her case a bird and a squirrel. She was able to perform magic, and she was a shape-shifter, able to transform at will from hag to maiden.

'What is your name?' the king said.

'My name, and the name of my offspring,' she said, 'will be given to this place. I am Macha, daughter of Sainrith mac Imbaith.'

Then she raced [against] the chariot. As the chariot reached the end of the field, she gave birth alongside it. She bore twins, a son and a daughter. The name Emain Macha, the Twins of Macha, comes from this.

FROM THE *TÁIN BÓ CUAILNGE*

Emhain Macha: Seat of Kings

In the Ulster Cycle, Emhain Macha was the royal seat of the mythical king Conchobar, the sacred place of assembly where the inauguration of Ulster kings took place. But archaeological evidence shows that this place was of great symbolic importance centuries before the time of the early medieval myths, for it has been identified with a long-lived

Navan Fort (reconstructed), Co. Armagh.

The goddess Macha shared some characteristics with Medbh, but it is Macha's triplefold persona that is her most striking feature, a property that linked her with the battle-furies, the Morrigán and the Badbh. Like Medbh, Macha was a goddess of sovereignty, and one of the great royal centres of northern Ireland, Emhain Macha, is named after her. Macha is presented in the stories as a three-in-one character whose origins are separate but were all merged into one multi-faceted persona. All three Machas, though, were clearly associated with sovereignty, fertility and the personification of

---

Iron Age site of Navan Fort in Co. Armagh. Here, in 94 BC (we know this so precisely thanks to a dendrochronological (tree-ring) date on the timbers), an enormous circular oaken temple-structure was built on raised ground, with a towering central post that could be seen for miles. The roof was thatched and the whole edifice was immediately and deliberately burnt down, perhaps as a sacrifice to the celestial gods.

Nearby, in the valley below, was a small lake, Loughnashade, into which four beautifully decorated ceremonial bronze trumpets had been placed as a religious offering. Perhaps they had been used in the ritual that accompanied the destruction of the temple, thus making a double sacrifice: of the building and the trumpets. Clearly Navan Fort dates to a much earlier period than the mythical Emhain Macha, but archaeological investigation has demonstrated the site's longevity as a place of major ceremonial significance for more than a millennium. One find from Iron Age Navan is especially significant: the skull of a Barbary Ape, brought all the way from North Africa as a splendidly exotic present to the lord of Navan.

Bronze Iron Age ceremonial trumpet, one of four ritually deposited in a lake near Navan Fort.

Schist plaque depicting three goddesses, from Roman Bath.

Ireland itself. One, like Medbh, was a warrior-ruler; another was the wife of King Nemedh and a prophetess (the name of the king is significant for it derives from the Celtic word *nemeton*, meaning 'sacred grove'); the third – the most complex and interesting – was a goddess married to a mortal man named Crunnchu.

This last Macha was inextricably linked with horses, and was undoubtedly a horse-goddess, like Epona and the Welsh mythic Rhiannon. It is she who is most fully described in the myths. She was the fleetest runner in the land and her swiftness led Crunnchu to lay a bet with the king that she could outrun his speediest chariot. Macha was heavily pregnant at the time but even so was forced to run the race; she won but died giving birth to twins. As she expired, she cursed the men of Ulster with a weakening spell, so that whenever they faced a crisis in battle they would be stricken with a weakness like that of a woman in labour for four days and nights. Macha's race identifies her as a horse-goddess. It is telling, too, that one of Cú Chulainn's two chariot-horses was named the Grey of Macha.

• FEDELMA: SPIRIT, SEER AND SHAMAN •

*The driver turned the chariot round. As they made to go back
to camp a young woman appeared before them. She had yellow
hair. She wore a dappled cloak with a gold pin, a hooded tunic
with red embroidery and shoes with gold buckles. Her face was
broad above and slender beneath, her eyebrows dark, and her
black eyelashes cast a shadow halfway down her cheek. Her
lips were of a Parthian red, inset with teeth like pearls. Her
hair was done up in three plaits…. In her hand was a weaver's
beam of white bronze inlaid with gold. Her eyes had triple
irises. The young woman was armed. Her chariot was drawn
by two black horses.*

FROM THE *TÁIN BÓ CUAILNGE*

The bloody finale of the great war between Ulster and Connacht, as
told in the Ulster Cycle, was predicted with great accuracy by one
of the strangest actors in the drama. At the start of the campaign,
while Medbh drove around in her chariot rallying her troops, a
young girl appeared before the queen and her army. Her appearance
was striking, as the quote above describes. When challenged by the
queen as to her identity, she replied that her name was Fedelma and
that she was a poet from Connacht. Of the many other questions
put to her, the most telling was 'Have you the *imbas forosnai*, the
Light of Foresight?' Fedelma replied that she had, and Medbh asked
her to prophesy the outcome of the war and the fate of her army.
Fedelma then gave the chilling response, in verse, that she saw the
army bathed in crimson and described the Ulster hero Cú Chulainn
as the means of Connacht's destruction.

But who or what was Fedelma? The clues lie in the way the
storyteller described her appearance. The emphasis on the number
three is significant: her triple-irised eyes showed that she was not
a normal human, but was touched by the Otherworld. Indeed, her
visual threeness may symbolize her ability to look into the past,

145

present and future, or into the three layers of the cosmos: the upper air, earth and underworld. Her speckled cloak, too, pronounces her status as a 'two-spirit' being, a title often conferred upon shamans because of their ability to travel between worlds. Clothing that was bi-coloured, that shimmered or was dappled, reflected this duality.

A principal function of a shaman was to be a seer, to predict the future, and this is exactly what Fedelma was doing. Her appearance as a warrior, armed and in a chariot is less easy to explain. Perhaps she was equipped like this because she was facing the evil that war brings, and thus reflected the moral, anti-war stance of the Christian cleric who wrote down the story. Fedelma's weaving-rod gives her a further dimension: she had the power to weave the thread of Medbh's destiny and to cut off Connacht's life-force when the gods demanded it.

• MAIDENS, MATRONS AND HAGS •

As they were there in the hostel, a woman appeared at the entrance, after sunset, and sought to be let in. As long as a weaver's beam, and as black, were her two shins. She wore a very fleecy striped mantle. Her beard reached to her knees, and her mouth was on one side of her head.
FROM 'DA DERGA'S HOSTEL'

We have already encountered the triadic Macha, the Morrígan and the Badbh, who could appear as humans or carrion birds, but also as any of the three stages of womanhood: maiden, mother or crone. In this way, a single entity could transcend fixed age and represent the totality of womanhood. In the tale of 'Da Derga's Hostel', Conaire Mór's doom is set when he is forced to give hospitality to a solitary woman despite his *geis* never to be alone with one. The terrifying hag he encounters has many supernatural 'tags': she crossed gender, she wears a bi-coloured cloak, and is of abnormal appearance.

Badbh and Macha, rich the store
Morrigán who dispenses confusion
compassers of death by the sword
noble daughters of Errimas.
FROM THE BOOK OF INVASIONS

A very famous encounter between a human ruler and a hag-goddess perhaps laid the foundations for early modern fairy tales of transformation, such as the story of the Frog Prince. It is contained within a very early origin myth – perhaps written down as early as the 5th century AD – in which the community known as the Ui Neill (the People of Niall) was founded. The founder of the dynasty was Niall of the Nine Hostages, and his rule is legitimized in the story by his encounter with the goddess of sovereignty, in the guise of a hag.

Niall and his brothers were out hunting and grew thirsty. They found a well guarded by a grotesque old crone, who offered each of them water in exchange for a kiss. They all recoiled in horror except

Pipe-clay model of Rhenish triple goddesses, from Bonn, Germany.

Imaging the Raven-goddess

On coins minted in the 2nd century BC by the Armorican (Breton) tribe of the Unelli, is the image of a galloping war-horse ridden by a huge carrion bird whose great curved talons dig into its back. Beneath the horse are a scorpion-like creature and a snake that both appear to be attacking it. It is tempting to see the ancestress of the Irish raven-goddesses in this strange scene. Could the mythology of the Irish shape-shifting battle-furies have sprung from a much earlier lost war-myth that may, itself, have been born from seeing carrion birds feeding off corpses on battlefields?

Gold Armorican Iron Age coin depicting a horse being ridden by a huge raven.

for Niall, who kissed her and then had sex with her. During their union, the hag transformed herself into a beautiful young girl (just as, in the Grimm's fairy tale, a kiss from a maiden caused the frog to morph into a handsome young prince). When Niall enquired her name, she told him she was Sovereignty. Niall duly became king, his rule endorsed by his marriage with the land of Ireland itself.

● WRONGED WIVES AND FLAWED WOMEN ●

And there was such an uproar in Ireland that there was no peace for Matholwch until he had avenged the disgrace he had suffered in Wales. His men took revenge by sending Branwen from her husband's chamber, and forcing her to cook for the court; and they had the butcher come to her every day, after he had chopped up meat, and give her a box on the ear.

FROM THE SECOND BRANCH OF THE *MABINOGI*

The Second Branch of the *Mabinogi* is often called 'Branwen', after its central female character. Despite being named as one of the greatest three women in Wales, Branwen herself is presented as a slightly soppy and ineffectual victim of male domination and aggression, and it is only once she is being mistreated at the court of her new husband (see p. 92) that the storyteller gives her character some substance. She rears a starling in the kitchen, teaches it to speak and tells it of her brother. Writing a letter to him about her situation, she ties it to the base of the starling's wings and instructs it to fly to Harlech. Brân's vengeful war inflicts huge casualties on Wales and Ireland. Full of sorrow at the destruction of two fine nations, Branwen dies of a broken heart.

Like Branwen, Rhiannon, the female 'hero' of the First Branch of the *Mabinogi* was mistreated and humiliated. Rhiannon's supernatural status is clear from her first appearance in the tale, dressed in shimmering gold; her mount, too, is a dazzling white horse, its colouring betraying its Otherworld origins. Lurking beneath Rhiannon's visible persona is a veiled divinity: on the occasion of her wedding, she greets each guest with a gift of precious jewelry, thus taking the role of the bountiful goddess of sovereignty. The weird punishment meted out to Rhiannon when she is wrongly accused of murdering and eating her son (having to act like a beast of burden and bear visitors on her back to the gates of the palace) may refer to another, probably earlier, strand of the Rhiannon myth, which identifies her as a goddess of horses.

> *'Maiden', said he, 'art thou a maiden?' 'I know not but that I am.'*
> *Then he took the magic wand and bent it. 'Step over this', said*
> *he, 'and if thou art a maiden, I shall know.' Then she stepped*
> *over the magic wand, and with that step she dropped a fine*
> *boy-child with rich yellow hair. The boy uttered a loud cry. After*
> *the boy's cry she made for the door, and thereupon dropped a*
> *small something, and before any could get a second glimpse of it,*
> *Gwydion took it and wrapped a sheet of silk around it, and hid it.*
> FROM THE FOURTH BRANCH OF THE *MABINOGI*

The Fourth Branch of the *Mabinogi*, often labelled 'Math' is steeped in magic, and the two women who dominate this mythic tale are flawed and negative: Arianrhod and Blodeuwedd, respectively the mother and wife of Lleu Llaw Gyffes. Arianrhod's lack of chastity and cruelty to her son are complicated by an extra, hidden facet of this story. For Math's magical wand, used to test virginity, is almost certainly a phallic symbol, the inference being that Arianrhod had sex with her uncle and became pregnant by him. This may explain her attempt to block Lleu's marriage and any chance of his having children. But in Celtic myth, children born as a result of incest reflected not just shame, but also heroic status. As in Classical myths, incest was endemic among the gods and any progeny so conceived was special, blessed by the gods. Both Math and Arianrhod were almost certainly closet divinities: Math's magical powers proclaim this, and so does Arianrhod's name 'Silver Wheel', a celestial epithet perhaps referring to the moon.

The second flawed woman to dog the life of Lleu was Blodeuwedd. A 'virtual' wife, she was conjured out of flowers, but the choice of flowers – broom, oak and meadowsweet – are telling, for the yellow broom is a simile frequently used in both Welsh and Irish myth to describe the hair of a young virgin, and the petals of both the oak and meadowsweet are white, symbols of purity. This makes Blodeuwedd's faithlessness ironic, but it is nevertheless almost expected because of her non-human nature: she is a wayward, amoral spirit-being, in some ways rather like Mary Shelley's created monster Frankenstein, or the robotic computer in Kubrick's *2001: A Space Odyssey*. Blodeuwedd's creator, Gwydion, was also the instrument of her destruction, though because she was not human, she could not be killed and thus by his magic was destined to haunt the world forever, no longer as a woman but an owl, symbol of night, sorrow and evil.

• EARLY GODDESSES IN TEXTS AND ARCHAEOLOGY •

Many of the goddesses who left their mark in the archaeological record or in the testimony of Classical writers on the Celts show distinct similarities with the supernatural females found in the later Irish and Welsh myths. Some were overtly bloodthirsty, wielding weapons and demanding human sacrifices. Others were apparently powerful but essentially peaceful. Like their mythic sisters, the earlier goddesses often possessed a close affinity with animals, whether horses, dogs or birds. This rich, if indirect, ancestry is especially clear in the Irish mythical warrior-women, such as Medbh and the Morrigán, who followed in the footsteps of war-goddesses worshipped in early Britain and Gaul.

Andraste

The 3rd-century AD writer Cassius Dio wrote of Boudica's plea to the goddess Andraste that she would triumph over the Romans in Britain in AD 60. Andraste needed human blood to appease her, and her will was shown to the Iceni rebel queen by means of a hare, which ran in a certain direction to indicate Andraste's support for the rebels' cause.

Despite such a sign, Boudica and her army were defeated, but not before three Roman cities and half a Roman legion had been destroyed. No certain image of Andraste survives in ancient British iconography. However, generic war-goddesses were depicted. Some northern Gallic coins issued by the Redones (around modern Rennes) depict a wild-haired naked horsewoman, brandishing weapons and screaming at the enemy.

A Silurian Goddess

Sometime in the 3rd century AD, a devotee set up a small sandstone statue of a local goddess (below) at Caerwent in south Wales, the capital city of the Silures. This tribe had bitterly opposed Roman domination for many years after the rest of southern Britain had been pacified, and was only subdued after a Roman legionary fortress was established at nearby Caerleon in about AD 75. The stone carving probably once stood in a temple, perhaps the one built near the Roman marketplace and town hall in Caerwent.

Sandstone statuette of a seated goddess, with yew-frond and berry, from Caerwent.

The name of this goddess is unknown, but the sculptor provided some information about her. She was depicted sitting in a high-backed chair, a mark of high status. She carried a piece of fruit or small loaf and what looks like the branch of a fir-tree. But instead, this latter object may represent a frond of yew, a symbol of longevity and rebirth (because of this tree's ability to regenerate itself from inside the trunk). If so, then the carving brings to mind Caer Yew-Berry, the spirit girlfriend of Oenghus, the Irish god of love.

Nerthus and Nehalennia

In his *Annals*, written at the end of the 1st century AD, Tacitus described an annual Germanic ceremony in honour of a fertility goddess called Nerthus, whose shrine was in a sacred grove upon a holy island. In preparation for her festival, all objects of iron had to be hidden away. The goddess was driven around her fields in a cart, draped with a cloth (in a ritual reminiscent of the ceremony of 'beating the bounds' that is still carried out in English parishes today

Bronze cult-wagon depicting stags, hunters, horsemen and a great central goddess holding a bowl of offerings. 7th century BC, from Strettweg, Austria.

to mark their physical limits). No one but her priest was allowed to touch the cloth or the vehicle. Afterwards, before being returned to her sanctuary, the wagon and the goddess were purified in a sacred lake by two slaves. But these slaves had touched something too holy for them to be allowed to live and so they were ritually drowned in Nerthus's lake. Although Nerthus was presented as an essentially benign deity, bringing prosperity to her farming community, she therefore had a dark side too, and demanded human sacrificial victims from her worshippers.

Like Nerthus, Nehalennia was a northern goddess: she belonged to Celto-German peoples living in what is now the Netherlands, near the North Sea coast. She was a goddess who protected merchant sailors carrying merchandise between Britain and Holland. Although not found in ancient literature, her identity is known from a rich assemblage of stone sculptures and inscriptions that survived the drowning of her temples by the encroachment of the sea.

Nehalennia is often depicted with marine imagery, such as boats or steering oars, and with symbols of bounty, such as baskets of fruit and bread. But her constant companion was a large hound, which is displayed on her monuments sitting close beside her, clearly part of her persona. The dog expressed the guardianship qualities of the goddess, and may also tell of her other role as a healer-deity. The Greek healer-god Asclepius was closely associated with dogs: live animals were kept in his sanctuary at Epidaurus, because of their perceived capacity to heal sick supplicants through their spittle.

A Breton Goose-goddess

A large late Iron Age bronze figurine from Dinéault near Rennes depicts a young battle-goddess. All that survive are her head, arms and feet, but the fingers of her right hand are curled as though gripping a spear-shaft. She wears a helmet, on top of which is a goose, its neck thrust out aggressively towards an enemy. The statuette probably represents a local protector-goddess, perhaps a tribal

Late Iron Age Bronze goose-goddess from Dinéault, Brittany.

guardian. Geese are known for their territoriality and their alertness in warning off intruders to property. In Iron Age society, these birds were revered as war-icons and their bodies were sometimes buried with warriors in graves. The cavalrymen depicted on the Gundestrup Cauldron wear bird-crested helmets, and these birds may have been geese – or ravens, who were particularly associated with battle-imagery in Celtic mythology.

8

LAND AND WATER: A SEETHE OF SPIRITS

After three days Uathach told Cú Chulainn that if he really
wanted to learn heroic deeds, he must go where Scáthach
was teaching her two sons Cúar and Cat, and give his hero's
salmon-leap up to the big yew-tree where she was resting.
FROM THE *TÁIN BÓ CUAILNGE*

Many stories told in Celtic myths attempted to make sense of the
world and natural phenomena. Spirits lurked in every feature of
the landscape. Each mountain, lake, stream, bog and tree had a life-
force whose origin lay in the supernatural world. This notion is akin
to the Roman belief that each place possessed a *genius loci*, the spirit
of place. For the Celts, the idea that the land was populated with
spirits was such a strong pulse in people's consciousness that their
myths, particularly in Ireland, contain a prominent perception that
the king's power rested with the goddess of sovereignty, the personification of the land itself, and that only by her acceptance of him
and her marriage to him could he rule successfully (see p. 165).

• TREES OF LIFE AND DEATH •

Superstitious natives believed that the ground often shook,
that groans rose from hidden caverns below, that yews were
uprooted and miraculously replanted, and that sometimes
serpents coiled about the oaks, which blazed with fire but did
not burn. Nobody dared enter this grove except the priest; and
even he kept out at midday, and between dawn and dusk – for
fear that the gods might be abroad at such hours.
LUCAN, *PHARSALIA* III, 417–422

17th–18th-century picture of Pliny's druidic ceremony of the oak and mistletoe.

In ancient Ireland, the oak, yew, ash and hazel were singled out for special veneration. Of these, the oak seems to have been the most sacred, probably because of its great size and longevity (like the yew). Oaks dominate rural landscapes even today and it is easy to see how, in a world without large buildings and towns, this tree would have been an integral part of the sacred, numinous landscapes of Ireland and Wales.

The earliest reference to the oak's religious significance appears in Pliny the Elder's *Natural History*, written in the 1st century AD, wherein he described a Druidic ritual in Gaul, centred around the Vallonia Oak, the most sacred of all trees. He recounts how a Druid would climb the oak on the sixth day of the waxing moon and cut down the mistletoe growing on it, catching it in a white cloth. Two white bulls were sacrificed and the mistletoe leaves and berries made up into a potion that magically cured all diseases and made barren animals fertile.

For the ancient Druids, then, oaks were deemed special, host of the curious parasitic mistletoe, which grows as bright green balls on apparently dead winter trees, its viscous white berries symbols of the moon, their sticky juice like semen. The sacred importance of oaks runs through many Irish and Welsh myths. In the Classical world, oaks were associated with sky-gods, and this link is also present in the Welsh story of Lleu, the Welsh god of light, who when attacked turned into an eagle and roosted in an oak.

Healing Mistletoe

The young man found in a peat bog in 1984 at Lindow Moss in Cheshire was sacrificed to the gods in the 1st century AD. He sustained savage blows to his head, and had his throat cut while being garrotted. His soft tissue was preserved (see image p. 195) because of the waterlogged, airless conditions in which he was buried, and so it was possible to examine his stomach-contents. He was found to have eaten a special kind of griddled bread, made from a variety of cereals and seeds, but including mistletoe pollen. Could this have been a sacred food, eaten to sanctify the offering to the spirit world, or was it intended as a symbolic healing agent, designed to ease his passage into the Otherworld?

Although usually regarded as poisonous, there is startling modern testimony to the curative powers of mistletoe. *The Times* reported in 2012 that John Edrich, a former England cricketer who was suffering from leukaemia, had his quality of life and life expectancy greatly enhanced by twice-weekly injections of mistletoe by a cancer specialist in Aberdeen. Apparently, the plant has the property of boosting the human immune system, and research is ongoing to see whether other cancer-sufferers could benefit from similar treatment.

According to Irish mythic traditions associated with kingship, oak trees were the focal point in places of assembly, such as Tara (Co. Meath) and Emhain Macha (Co. Armagh), where the inauguration of the kings took place. In the collection of prose tales known as The History of Places, trees, especially oaks, were perceived as sources of wisdom (this ties in with the etymology of the word 'Druid', accepted as meaning something like 'the wisdom of the oak'). The mythical royal seat of Emhain Macha, as we have seen, had an enormous circular oaken structure; at its centre was a massive, towering timber upright so tall that it could be seen for miles. This must have represented a living sacred oak.

A Magical Welsh Oak

An oak grows between two lakes,
very dark is the sky and the valley.
Unless I am mistaken
this is because of Lleu's flowers.

An oak grows on a high plain,
rain does not wet it, heat no longer melts it;
it sustained one who possesses nine-score attributes.
In its top is Lleu Llaw Gyffes.

ENGLYNS SUNG BY GWYDION TO LLEU, IN THE FOURTH BRANCH OF THE MABINOGI

Lleu Llaw Gyffes was a hero of the Fourth Branch of the *Mabinogi.* The story contains a curious episode in which a magic oak had centre-stage. When mortally wounded by his wife Blodeuwedd's lover, Lleu gave an unearthly screech and, turning into an eagle, flew up into the air and vanished. Lleu's uncle Gwydion had always championed his nephew, and was mystified by his disappearance. Having wandered through central Wales in search of Lleu for some time, Gwydion came to a peasant's house where he stayed the night.

Sacred Groves

Classical literature and inscriptions on coins are testament to the veneration of trees in ancient Gaul, for the names of certain tribes reflect tree-symbolism. The Eburones were the 'Yew Tribe', the Lemovices the 'People of the Elm'. Groves of trees had a particular sanctity in Celtic Gaul and Britain prior to the Roman conquest. Tacitus, Lucan and other writers refer to Gallo-British sacred groves where spirits lurked and where human sacrifices were perpetrated. The hare that the British queen Boudica released to divine the will of the British victory-goddess Andraste was set to run in a grove.

It transpired that the swineherd of the household had been having trouble with his sow, which disappeared each night. Next day, Gwydion set off to find the sow; she finally halted under an oak where she gorged herself on maggots and decaying flesh. There was an eagle in the tree; whenever the bird shook its feathers, it rained down a shower of maggots and fragments of rotting flesh. Recognizing that the eagle was his transformed nephew Lleu, Gwydion sang him three variations of an *englyn* (a magical poem) to entice him down.

The song mentions the oak in which the eagle perched, and also 'Lleu's flowers', clearly a reference to Blodeuwedd, his wife of flowers. After the third stanza of the poem, the bird landed on Gwydion's knee; the magician struck it with his magical staff and Lleu turned back into human shape. But the rotting flesh and worms had taken their toll: the hapless man was nothing but skin and bone. Eventually, after a year of medical care, Lleu recovered.

The role of the oak in this Welsh myth is not immediately apparent, but the tree seems to have acted as a guardian, enabling the wounded Lleu to stay suspended between life and death, in a tree that reached towards the sky, until he could be rescued and brought back to human life. The eagle may have represented the freed spirit of the dead man, caught in limbo, unable to enter the world of the dead.

• THE WATER-MYTHS •

Tir na n'og, the Land of the Young, was as sweet as Elysium, as vivid as Nirvana, as desirable as Valhalla, as green and sunny as Eden. All souls aimed to gain this eternal heaven and every time one of the Atlantic waves, the 'white horses', folded over onto the shore of the Land of the Young, another spirit received permission to enter.

FROM THE FENIAN CYCLE

Given their ocean-girt island home, it is no surprise that the Irish venerated a sea-god. His name was Manannán mac Lir, 'Son of the Sea'. He had a close counterpart in Wales, with a corresponding name: Manawydan son of Llŷr. But we know most about the Irish god. Because his sea-realm surrounded the land of Ireland, Manannán was revered as its protector. He was particularly connected with the myth of the Happy Otherworld, believed to exist on islands far out at sea. A 7th-century text, *The Voyage of Bran* tells the story of a mortal man lured to these islands by sweet music whose sound carried across the water. Bran, the hero, set sail for the island, with his three foster-brothers and 27 warriors. While on the sea-voyage, Bran met Manannán, riding his sea-chariot pulled by the 'white horses' of the turbulent sea. He wore a magical cloak, which, like the sea itself, sparkled with light and assumed many shimmering colours.

Both Manannán and his Welsh counterpart Manawydan were not only sea-gods but also lords of magic, wisdom, trickery and craftsmanship. The Irish god was able to help Lugh, the Irish god of light, defeat the monstrous Fomorians. He did this by using

Boann's River

Given that a key function of myth is to explain features of the natural world, it comes as no surprise that legends have been woven around the major rivers of Britain and Ireland, with most given female identities. In England, the Romano-Britons personified the Thames as the goddess Tamesis, and the Severn as Sabrina. In the north, Verbeia was the goddess of the river Wharfe. The most famous river in Irish myth was the great Boyne, named after a goddess, Boann.

The story of Boann is related in the topographical History of Places. At one level, the tale can be interpreted within the context of the familiar Christian theme of pagan promiscuity and feminine waywardness. Boann was the errant wife of a water-spirit named Nechtan, who possessed a well that Boann was forbidden to visit. As almost always happened with such taboos or prohibitions, she disobeyed him and, in his rage, the water in his well boiled up into a torrent and engulfed her. She became the river Boyne. In another tale, Boann had a secret liaison with one of the greatest Irish gods, the Daghdha. The fruit of their union was Oenghus, the divine patron of lovers.

Bronze statuette of the Gallic river-goddess Sequana, of the Seine.

Gold model boat from Broighter, Co. Derry, Ireland. 1st century BC.

magic to create a boat that obeyed the thoughts of its crew and was powered without oars or sails; a horse that could swim as well as it could gallop; and 'Fragarach', a formidable sword capable of slicing through any armour. In Welsh mythology Manawydan was equally gifted: his major roles were as a magical metalsmith and a farmer. It may be that, in the particular attributes of Manawydan, we can see glimpses of a very early foundation myth that sought to explain the origins of both cultivation and smithing.

The Power of Water: Swan Lake

Here on Derravaragh's lonely wave
for many a year to be your watery home,
no power of Lir or druid can now ye save
from endless wandering on the lonely foam.

FROM THE BOOK OF INVASIONS

The transformation of young maidens into swans at lakes is a persistent motif in Irish mythology, and it seems as though an aquatic location was necessary in order for the shape-shifting to be successful. The tale of Oenghus and the swan-girl Caer is a prime example (see pp. 69–70). Another story involves Manannán mac Lir the sea god. His children had a wicked stepmother named Eva. In her jealousy, she cast a spell on them and turned them into swans, first luring them to a lake and then invoking a Druid's help to achieve their enchantment.

A condition of their eventual release from bird-shape was that they should first spend 300 years in each of three locations. However, the curse would only be lifted when a northern prince married a southern Irish girl of royal birth and when the swan-childen of Lir heard the tolling of a bell. Both these terms are significant: the marriage suggests union between the north and south of Ireland and particularly, perhaps, the ending of the feud between Ulster and Connacht; the bell was the 'voice' of Christianity, signifying the end of paganism and the adoption of the new Christian monotheism. The story, alas, had no happy ending. True, the spell was eventually lifted from the swan-children, but by then they were ancient crones; they died almost at once and a priest named Kemoc gave them a Christian burial.

The Paps of Anu, Rathmore, Co. Kerry, thought to be the breasts of the Irish founder-goddess Anu in early Irish mythology.

• SOVEREIGNTY, SACRAL KINGSHIP AND THE LAND •

One of the more powerful recurrent images of Irish myth is the personification of Ireland as a goddess. Pairs of hills were known variously as 'the breasts of the Morrígan' or the 'Paps of Anu' (or Danu, a founder-goddess of the land). In order for the land to prosper, there had to be a ritual marriage between the goddess and the mortal king of Ireland. If the earthly ruler was generous, the land would flourish; if niggardly, the deity would withdraw her beneficence and the land would languish until there was a new king.

As a sign that he was an acceptable mate, the goddess would hand the new king a cup of wine, to symbolize her pledge that under her patronage Ireland would be a land of plenty. The eponymous goddess of Ireland, Ériu, was one divine wine-giver. Another (as suggested by her name 'She Who Intoxicates') was Medbh, the queen-goddess of Connacht: she consorted with nine mortal kings, and for this she was denounced by her Christian chroniclers. In a pagan context, however, her 'promiscuity' ensured the continued fertility of the land.

Gallo-Roman Divine Partners

A recurrent relief group in indigenous Gallic cult-iconography depicts a
male and female, side by side. They are presented as equal partners, and
are equal in size. Where epigraphic evidence is present, the male often
has a Roman name but his partner a local one, sometimes containing
allusions to rivers or other features in the landscape, as if her persona
were defined by these local associations. Two widely venerated pairs of
Gaulish deities that show this are Mercury and Rosmerta, and Apollo and
Sirona. This pattern of naming would seem to suggest that it was the
goddess who was rooted in the land, while the god had a more flexible
and versatile nature, as well as being regarded as imported from outside.

Rosmerta's name can be translated as 'The Good Provider', aligning
her firmly with the same attributes as the Irish sovereignty goddess. On
her images, she frequently carries symbols of the earth's prosperity and
wellbeing: a cornucopia or a miniature house on a long pole that might
represent hearth and home. Sirona's name means 'Star', but despite
the suggestion that she was a celestial divinity, her imagery and context
show her to have been above all a goddess of healing. Stone and bronze
carvings depicting Apollo and Sirona were associated with Gallic healing
spring sanctuaries. Apollo himself was both a healer and a god of light,
so Sirona's partnership with him is appropriate.

Gallo-Roman stone carving of the divine partners Mercury and Rosmerta,
from Glanum, southern France.

Marrying the Mare

In 1185 Gerald of Wales (Giraldus Cambrensis) recorded a medieval royal inauguration ceremony of sacral kingship undergone by new rulers of Ulster. Curiously, the mythical marriage between the mortal king and the goddess of sovereignty is given a new twist, for in Gerald's testimony the symbolic union was between the human king and a white mare. For the 'wedding', the king played the part of a stallion. Afterwards, though, the mare was slain and her flesh cooked in a cauldron. Gerald paints a somewhat grisly picture of the king-elect seated in a bath containing the broth and meat of the mare while he ate and drank the boiled remains of his 'queen'.

This story was probably either fabricated or embroidered by its Christian chronicler. Yet it contains hints at earlier connections between horses and sovereignty-goddesses: Macha had strong equine associations and, in Wales, we might see a veiled sacral kingship tale in the First Branch of the *Mabinogi*, where Pwyll, king of Narberth, caught a first sight of his queen, Rhiannon, riding her sparkling white mare.

This system of partnership between human and divine was known in Irish tradition as sacral kingship, and was a foundation-stone of early Irish mythic literature. As a concept, it is not all that far removed from the much later British divine right of kings, wherein a monarch anointed by the Church was regarded as having been granted divine sanction, though this could still unravel if the king were seen to rule unwisely.

It is possible that the roots of sacral kingship lay in religious symbolism that can be traced back to the Roman period in Western Europe: certain sculptures depict divine couples wherein the woman carries emblems of fertility, such as a cornucopia (horn of plenty) while the man holds a cup or small pot. This is very clear on a stone carving from Glanum in southern France (see image opposite).

• ANCESTRAL LANDSCAPES AND COLLIDING PASTS •

*Long ago in Erin, when the people of Danu were defeated by
the Milesians, they had to go into the hills and mountains,
where they built themselves vast palaces inside the hills.*

FROM THE BOOK OF INVASIONS

Permeating the myths of Ireland was the idea of a tangible
Otherworld in which the spirits dwelt. This invisible realm could
be accessed in various ways (across the sea, through rivers or caves)
and was thought to be located in a range of places, including
islands. Central to this Otherworld were the *sídhe*, mounds in the
landscape that were identified in the myths as dwelling-places of the
gods. What seems to have happened is that ancient Irish Neolithic
passage-graves, such as Newgrange and Knowth, were claimed as
sídhe, even though they were built as tombs several millennia earlier
than the medieval prose tales. It is easy to see why such links were
made, for the ancient burial monuments, particularly the Boyne
Valley tombs, are impressive features of the landscape. Not only are
they large and striking, but they were also highly decorative, as if
indeed they were the abodes of the old gods.

The original builders of Newgrange constructed a façade
of gleaming white quartz speckled with black granodiorite, to
create a shimmering, dazzling wall of shifting colour. Inside these
massive stone tombs were slabs ornamented with strange designs.
Newgrange had an elaborate 'roof-box', a slit below the roof at the
entrance that allowed the sun at dawn on the midwinter solstice to
flood down the passage to the end-chamber, as if to summon the
dead with a clarion-call of light. No wonder such fantastic monuments were deemed incapable of being the work of ancestral human
hands and beliefs.

The roof-box over the entrance to the Neolithic passage-grave at Newgrange, Co. Meath, Ireland during the midwinter solstice.

Tara

The royal place of assembly at Tara in Co. Meath was steeped in myth. It was reputedly the seat of inauguration for both legendary and historical kings. The evidence for both royal legend and reality at Tara is based on medieval literature, including the mythic prose tales of the 8th–12th centuries AD and earlier historical documents including law-tracts.

169

A Royal Tara Legacy

One sound piece of archaeological evidence linking Tara to an early historical king is a funerary commemoration on an ogham stone found there. Ogham was an Irish linear script consisting of grouped horizontal strokes along a vertical edge, each individual combination of strokes forming a letter. This tombstone commemorates Mac Caírthinn, an early king of Leinster, whose name appears in a 7th-century law-tract.

One of the most famous 'Tara' finds from the early medieval period is the so-called 'Tara Brooch' (found not at Tara itself but at nearby Bettystown). The jewel, made of gilded silver, consisted of a ring-shaped brooch, inlaid with glass, enamel and amber, and covered with engraved and filigree ornament. It measured 4.6 cm (2 in.) in diameter, and was clearly worn as a cloak-clasp by someone of extremely high rank. Could this unique object once have decorated a mantle belonging to a high king of Tara?

Aerial view of Tara, the Royal Place of Assembly in Co. Meath, Ireland. The monuments date to the Neolithic and Bronze Age.

Tara is of huge archaeological significance, with a whole range of ancient monuments. But what is most striking about the site is that its reputation, as a ceremonial centre where high kings of Ireland were sworn in, is based almost entirely on a sacred monumental landscape that pre-dates the early medieval Irish mythic world by thousands of years. This ritual place contains prehistoric tombs, henges, linear embankments and standing stones, all of which were woven into legend. The first enclosure at Tara dates to the 4th millennium BC, followed by later Neolithic passage graves (similar to Newgrange), such as the 'Mound of the Hostages'. Bronze Age communities built round barrows and deposited gold treasure here.

• THE STONE OF FÁL •

In the early medieval period, prehistoric landmarks were embellished and incorporated into contemporary monuments, thus binding this ritual landscape to mytho-historical phases of the site. At one of these complexes was the Stone of Fál, a megalithic standing stone that was given a prominent place as a shrieking stone in the mythology of kingly inauguration. (The stone would give a great cry when touched by the rightful new king.)

Conaire Mór was a mythical Irish king. Like others, he had to undergo a series of trials by ordeal in order to establish his credentials as an appropriate ruler: the first of these was to mount a chariot that immediately tilted up and expelled any non-legitimate claimants and whose horses would attack him. The claimant had to don a mantle reposing within the chariot: if he was not the rightful king, the cloak was far too large. Next Conaire had to drive the chariot between two stones; if he were not acceptable, the stones would narrow the gap and not allow him through except sideways on. Finally, at the head of the chariot-course the Stone of Fál was waiting to screech against the axle of a legitimate king's chariot. The

Standing stone, said to be the Stone of Fál, at the Hill of Tara, Co. Meath, Ireland.

stone was clearly meant as a phallic symbol, a sign of the rightful ruler's right to marry the goddess of sovereignty and cause the land to prosper.

• SEASONAL RITUALS •

'No man will travel this country,' she said, 'who hasn't gone sleepless from Samhain, when the summer goes to its rest, until Imbolc, when the ewes are milked at spring's beginning; from Imbolc to Beltine at the summer's beginning and from Beltine to Brón Trogain (Lughnasadh), earth's sorrowing autumn.'
FROM THE *TÁIN BÓ CUAILNGE*

All over the temperate world, people acknowledge, celebrate and sanctify the changes between the seasons. From the Christian festival of Easter to January's Shetland Viking fire festival of Up Helly Aa, seasons play a fundamental role in the calendars of rural peoples and nowhere more so than in farming communities. In Celtic Ireland, four major seasonal ceremonies marked the different stages in the arable and pastoral year. Samhain was celebrated at the end of October/ beginning of November, at the interface between the old and new Celtic years. Like its successor Hallowe'en, Samhain was a dangerous time of 'not being' when the world stood still and spirits left their Otherworld home to roam among the living.

In origin, Samhain was linked to the pastoral calendar and was probably connected with gathering in herds of cattle and sheep from open pasture for the winter and selecting those destined for culling or for winter feeding and breeding. Samhain was closely linked with Tara and it was at this sacred and perilous time that many assemblies and kingly inaugurations took place, so that they could be blessed by the wandering gods.

The early spring festival was Imbolc: it was celebrated in early February and was linked to lambing and the milk-production of ewes. The name meant purification or cleansing, and this may be linked with the whiteness of milk but also, perhaps, with the need to check the health of beasts after their winter confinement, when infections could easily run riot among flocks and herds. Imbolc was especially associated with Brigit, a pagan Irish goddess in charge of dairies. Brigit was transformed into a saint in the early Christian period, but she still kept her responsibilities for the production of milk, butter and cream.

The two other Celtic festivals marked the beginning and end of summer. Beltane (or Beltine) was a fire festival and, like many solar ceremonies, was celebrated both in thanksgiving for the arrival of warm weather and sunshine and to ensure that the sun would always return to ripen the crops. The Beltane ceremonies took place on May 1st in Ireland and Scotland. Fires were lit by the Druids in sacred places, such as Tara, and herds of cattle were driven between

An Ancient Gaulish Calendar

In 1897, fragments of a large sheet-bronze tablet were discovered deliberately buried in a field north of Coligny in central France. The pieces were part of a huge inscribed five-year ritual lunar calendar written in Roman characters, and probably dating to the 1st–3rd centuries AD, but written in Gallic. The calendar lists sacrificial and other sacred events, and divides each 28-day month into fortnights according to the waxing and waning of the moon: the first fortnight was the most active and was divided from the second by the Gaulish word Atenoux. One of the most significant words in the inscription is 'Samonios', the same word as Samhain. This indicates that the Celtic festivals were by no means confined to the western Celtic fringes, but were originally celebrated over a much wider region including Gaul.

The Coligny Calendar had been a valuable and very sacred object, used to predict natural events and to plan religious ceremonies. So why was it deliberately broken into pieces and buried? Perhaps it had become redundant but was too greatly charged with spirit-force for the metal to be melted down and re-used. Or maybe the shattered fragments represent the results of persecution, and the perceived need of local clergy to maintain the calendar's secrets by hiding it and making it impossible to read (much as we cut up bank cards today).

Part of the Coligny Calendar, from Ain, France.

pairs of bonfires in order to purify them. This was a ritual act but it also served the practical purpose of burning off dead skin and cleansing the animals of parasites.

According to the medieval Irish texts, the first Druid to light a Beltane fire was called Mide. His fires spread all over Ireland, and so he incurred the jealous wrath of fellow Druids. Mide responded by cutting out the tongues of his adversaries and burning them, thus ridding them of their power of speech and their ability to curse or cast spells over him. A hidden Beltane festival may be identified in the Welsh mythic tradition, too, for it was at this time of year that magical things happened: it was at May-eve, for example, that Pryderi, son of Rhiannon and Pwyll, disappeared from his mother's side and magically reappeared far away at the house of Teyrnon, lord of Gwent Iscoed.

The final seasonal festival was Lughnasadh, celebrated in August to mark the ending of the summer period and the harvest. As the name suggests, this late-summer ceremony was associated with Lugh, the god of light and craftsmanship, who founded Lughnasadh to honour his mother Tailtu. Like Samhain, this feasting occasion was chosen for important ritual and political assemblies at royal courts such as Tara and Emhain Macha. All these seasonal ceremonies had in common their celebration at times of change, liminal periods that were deemed risky because transformation was perceived as fraught with danger and heavily influenced by a capricious band of untamed spirits whose power needed to be both venerated and contained.

Counterparts to the old Celtic farming festivals are celebrated in modern times in Britain and the western world. We still acknowledge May Day (Calan Mai in Wales). The Harvest Festival is an important event in the Christian Church's year. Hallowe'en (and the Christian All Souls Day) mark the coming of winter darkness and occur precisely at the same time as Samhain. Perhaps only Imbolc has not survived into the present.

HEAVEN AND HELL:
PARADISE AND THE UNDERWORLD

Delightful is the land beyond all dreams!
Beyond what seems to thee most fair –
rich fruits abound the bright year round
and flowers are found of hues most rare'.
FROM 'OISIN AND THE LAND OF FOREVER YOUNG'
IN THE FENIAN CYCLE

A key aspect of the human condition is a need to come to terms with death and to explore questions concerning what happens to us when we die. Is death the end or can we expect some kind of after-life? If so, is it conduct-related? If we have lived a good life, can we expect a reward in Heaven? Do the evil go to Hell? What are Heaven and Hell, anyway, and where can they be found? Do we hang on to our physical selves in any form? Are we reunited with loved ones in the next world? Given the preoccupation with these concerns, it is to be expected that some of the principal elements of myths throughout the world are descriptions of Otherworlds.

In some cultures, Heaven and Hell are intimately linked with the best and worst of human life. The Biblical Hell is full of fire and the torments of everlasting burning. But for the ancient Norse, while Valholl (Valhalla), the feasting-hall of Oðin, was warm, Hell was eternal cold, a wretched, shadowy place cut off from the human world by the river Gioll (similar to the Styx of Classical myth). At the heart of Christian notions of Heaven is the promise of intimacy with God. For many other religious traditions, a good afterlife involves all the best of the human experience with none of its nastiness.

For the Celts, the upside of the Otherworld (which did not have two separate and contrasting realms similar to a Heaven and a Hell)

A Gallic feast, as imagined in later times.

was an everlasting party, involving feasting, hunting and gaming. The downside was the potential for encounters with inimical spirits and monstrous beings, the spawn of nightmares. Living beings who had the temerity to penetrate the Otherworld while still tied to the human world (as did the Irish heroes Cú Chulainn and Finn), underwent the greatest risk of meeting something horrible. For the Celts, life after death demanded the retention of a physical body, with its digestion system intact. How else could the dead enjoy their great hunks of roast meat and tankards of liquor?

According to the traditions of the Sámi peoples living in northern Scandinavia and Siberia, the dead are believed to inhabit an underworld in which they walk upside-down in the footsteps of the living, in a mirror-image of life on earth. It paints an extraordinarily attractive picture of life after death: bodies are retained and direct links maintained with the material world; yet everything is, literally, turned on its head in a parallel universe whose borders can seldom be permeated except in one direction. The only way that this Otherworld is represented on earth is via spirits and shamans, and it can be accessed at specific 'fault-lines': islands, rapids, caves, rock-fissures and piles of stones, where local communities come to make sacrifices.

The Sámi vision of the afterlife, and access to the spirit-world, has much in common with beliefs about death in Celtic mythology. A combination of archaeological evidence, Classical literature and early medieval Irish and Welsh texts provide a view of a vividly tangible Otherworld populated by dead ancestors and the gods. Even the access-points, where the spirits could best be approached, were similar: special places in the landscape redolent with spiritual force. Water was key to Celtic perceptions of the Otherworld, perhaps because of the reflective properties that cause the world to be repeated visually, but reversed, on its surface.

It was at the festival of Samhain, at the edge of winter, that the world of humans was most at risk from the inhabitants of the world beyond: the boundaries were suspended and the spirits could prowl among the living, to their good or detriment depending on the character of the individual phantom. Now the dread female battle-furies could roam, washing the arms of warriors at a ford (symbolic of a pathway between worlds), and prophesying who would next die on the field of war. It was at Samhain, the time of 'not being', that living Celtic heroes, such as Finn and Cú Chulainn, were able to enter the world of the dead whilst still alive.

● COLOUR CODING ●

And of all the hounds he had seen in the world, he had never seen dogs of this colour – they were a gleaming shining white, and their ears were red. And as the whiteness of the dogs shone so did the redness of their ears.

FROM THE FIRST BRANCH OF THE *MABINOGI*

Waterfall at Great Langdale, Cumbria. Rapids and tumbling water were perceived to be access-points to the Otherworld.

Beings from the Otherworld who interfered with the lives of living people betrayed their presence by various coded messages that would have been deeply familiar to hearers of mythic tales. We have already encountered the most striking, which was colour-imagery: particularly white and red, sometimes combined. Both Ireland and Wales possessed traditions of white, red-eared animals, particularly dogs, that belonged to the gods. Arawn, king of the Welsh Otherworld, had a pack of white hunting-dogs with red ears whom Pwyll, lord of Arberth, encountered at the beginning of the Mabinogion. Allusion by storytellers to such creatures would have the immediate effect of sending a frisson of pleasurable horror down the spines of their listeners, who would sit back, waiting for something momentous and perhaps disastrous to happen.

In Irish myth, white boars erupted into unsuspecting earthworld from the nether regions and lured human hunters to their doom. In 'Culhwch and Olwen', the magical boars whom Olwen's father commanded Culhwch to overcome had silver bristles that glittered like steel. The fearsome battle-goddess, the Morrigán, appeared to Cú Chulainn as a red woman, red-haired and red-eyebrowed, driving a chariot pulled by a red horse with one leg (this 'impossible' abnormality yet another sign of its Otherworld origins). In another of her many manifestations, the Morrigán appeared to Cú Chulainn as a hornless red heifer. Colour gave substance to written or spoken tales; it evoked images and sent messages: white was the colour of bleached bones and bloodless corpses; red was the colour of blood and wounds.

A further instance of visual coding was that of variegation: stripes, stipples or speckling. Holy men and women wore dappled clothing to signify their dual nationalities: as members of both the realms of the living and the dead. Such a one was the Irish prophetess Fedelma, described in the *Táin Bó Cuailnge* as clad in a speckled cloak, when she appeared to Queen Medbh and prophesied her defeat at the hands of Cú Chulainn. The blind Druid Mog Ruith, who challenged the magical powers of the Ulster king Cormac with his own, also wore a dappled cloak, of feathers, with which he could fly between worlds.

• LIFE AFTER DEATH •

[The Druids] hold that the soul of a dead man does not descend to the silent, sunless world of Hades, but becomes reincarnate elsewhere; if they are right, death is merely a point of change in perpetual existence.
LUCAN, *PHARSALIA* I, 454–58

Classical writers such as Caesar and Lucan who described the customs of the ancient Gallic Celts, spoke of their perceptions concerning rebirth after death. The testimony of these authors can be interpreted in two ways. In one, people took on other physical bodies and re-inhabited the material world (this is taught also by the Greek philosopher–mathematician Pythagoras, and Hinduism). In the other, people retained their own bodies, but were rejuvenated in a parallel Otherworld (akin to the traditions of the Sámi). Archaeological evidence and early medieval Irish and Welsh mythic literature combine to suggest that it was the second view of life after death that prevailed in Celtic cosmologies.

When Pwyll and Arawn, lord of Annwfn (the Welsh Otherworld), exchanged realms for a year and a day (see p. 81), Arawn laid down two injunctions upon Pwyll: the first that he should not have sexual intercourse with Arawn's wife; the second was that he should kill Arawn's Otherworld rival Hafgan. Pwyll agreed to obey each of these commands and, when led to Arawn's realm, found a glittering court, full of gold, jewels and silk, and tables groaning with sumptuous food and drink. Arawn's beautiful wife was puzzled and distressed that her 'husband' did not share her bed, but Pwyll kept faith with his agreement.

It seems strange that Arawn could not fight his own battles for Otherworld supremacy, but herein lies an important aspect of Otherworld beings: they were physically insubstantial, weak, and lacked the robust energy of living mortals. At the end of the year-and-a-day, Pwyll found and slew Hafgan, and returned to his earthly kingdom of Narberth, to find that, according to earth-time, he had not been away at all. But Pwyll's men did observe a change in him since his sojourn in the spirit-world: they marvelled at how gracious and generous he had become, even more so than before his Otherworld adventure.

• THE CAULDRON OF REBIRTH •

I will give you a cauldron, and the property of the cauldron is that if you throw into it one of your men who is killed today, then by tomorrow he will be as good as ever except that he will not be able to speak.

FROM THE SECOND BRANCH OF THE *MABINOGI*

The Daghdha (or 'Good God') was responsible for the fertility of Ireland and, as such, he had a string of paramours, including Boann, goddess of the Boyne. The Daghdha had a range of magical implements, and among the most important were a huge club and a cauldron. One end of the club took life and the other restored it. But his cauldron represented the everlasting prosperity of the land, for it was a cauldron of regeneration, capable of providing a constant supply of food that never dwindled.

The Second Branch of the *Mabinogi* tells the tale of a magical cauldron of rebirth, the property of Brân the Blessed. It had the ability to resurrect soldiers slain in battle so well that they were as good as new the next day and, indeed, were able to fight even more bravely than before. But there was a downside to this resurrection-vessel, because the warriors placed in it were reborn without the capacity to speak. This means, in effect, that they were zombies, undead souls who had been lent back to earth-life merely to fight.

Speech was highly valued by the Celts, as the essence of what it was to be human. Oratory and poetry were cornerstones of communities, for the power of words was more important even than war-craft, and bards and prophets enjoyed the highest rank. The audience of this tale would realize that the men reborn in Brân's cauldron were dumb because they still belonged to the world of the dead, and, pawns of divine will, were only briefly restored to fight.

Imaging the Magic Cauldron

It is rare that a piece of archaeological evidence appears to provide a direct comparison with myth. But, despite being produced in the 1st century BC, so much earlier than the written myths, the icon-rich Gundestrup Cauldron may do just that (see also pp. 28, 29, 122, 140). One of the most striking of its panels (below) depicts what appears to be a scene remarkably similar to the Welsh tale of Brân's cauldron.

The panel consists of an upper and lower register. The lower frieze depicts a procession of foot soldiers facing left, all but one of whom bears a sword and an oblong shield; the last one (the only

Inner plate of the Gundestrup Cauldron, Denmark, depicting the restoration of warriors to life in a cauldron.

Arthur's Cauldron

The Welsh prose tale 'The Spoils of Annwn' was compiled in written form in the late 13th or early 14th century. It tells of a magical Otherworld vessel, made of dazzling bronze and studded with precious stones. The cauldron was capricious: it would never boil food for a coward, and it required the breath of nine virgins to heat its broth. Typical of the Otherworld, it gave with one 'hand' and took away with the other. When Arthur embarked upon a brazen cauldron-rustling expedition, he managed to acquire the cauldron, but most of his forces were wiped out in the attempt. This vessel was specifically known by the term *Peir Annwfn*, 'Otherworld Cauldron'.

An ancient cauldron, made in the 8th century BC and thrown into Llyn Fawr in South Wales, along with another more fragmentary vessel and other treasure, is strongly reminiscent of the *Peir Annwfn*, for it has numerous domed rivets all over it, far more than were needed to hold its metal sheets together. At night, lit only by the hearth-fire, this once brightly shining red-gold cauldron would have glowed and reflected the flames, and the rivets would have glittered like diamonds. Perhaps the chance discovery, in early medieval times, of such ancient objects as the Llyn Fawr Cauldron might have inspired storytellers to weave old imagery into new myths. If they came from lakes or pools, they might well have seemed to belong to the Otherworld.

Cauldron (one of a pair) offered to the spirit of the lake at Llyn Fawr in about 700 BC.

warrior on this register with a helmet) has a long sword but no shield. Behind him are three trumpeters, each one bearing a *carnyx*, a long-stemmed war-trumpet, the bell of each surmounted by a snarling boar's head. At the left-hand end of the panel, the leading infantryman faces a rearing hound and an enormous human figure, more than twice the size of the soldiers; he is in the act of thrusting one of the warriors face-down into a large vat or cauldron. The upper register depicts four cavalrymen facing right whose horses ride high-stepping, dressage-style, away from the cauldron. Each armed horseman wears a helmet ornamented with animal-symbols. Leading the mounted warriors is a ram-horned serpent.

It is very tempting to interpret this scene on the Gundestrup Cauldron as analogous to the rebirth episode in the Mabinogion. If this is correct, then the infantrymen may represent dead warriors lining up for resurrection in the magical cauldron of regeneration, their revivification represented by their increased status as cavalrymen. The hybrid snake may be a two-spirit, shamanic creature whose mingled form depicts its capacity to lead souls between worlds. It appears, too, that the foot soldiers on the lower register have their eyes shut, as if in death, whereas the horsemen's eyes are open.

Eating with the Dead

Seven doors had Mac Da Thó's hostel, and seven entrances and seven hearths and seven cauldrons. Each cauldron contained beef and salted pork, and as each man passed by he thrust the flesh-fork into the cauldron.
FROM THE ULSTER CYCLE STORY 'MAC DA THÓ'S PIG'

The Irish Book of Invasions describes how the divine race, the Tuatha Dé Danann, were ousted from power by the next wave of invaders, the Gaels (or Celts). The Tuatha Dé Danann did not disappear from Ireland altogether, but they left the world of humans in order to inhabit the Otherworld, dwelling in a series of mounds,

Neolithic burial chamber at Tinkinswood, perhaps seen by early Welsh Celts as the abode of the spirits. South Glamorgan, South Wales.

or *sídhe*, beneath the earth. So rather than there being a single god of the Otherworld, there were many, each of whom had a *bruiden* or feasting-hall. These hostels were places of sumptuous hospitality, where the dead could eat and drink all day and all night, where liquor flowed constantly, and there were everlasting supplies of pork, because each day slaughtered pigs were resurrected, killed and roasted anew.

• SENDING OFF IN STYLE: THE FUNERARY BANQUET •

Although Gaul is not a rich country, funerals there are splendid and costly. Everything the dead man is thought to have been fond of is put on the pyre, including even animals. Not long ago slaves and dependants known to have been their masters' favourites were burned with them at the end of the funeral.
CAESAR, *DE BELLO GALLICO* 6.19

186

The strong message of the myths is a belief in a tangible life after death, an afterlife that mirrored all that was good about life on earth. Some funerary practices of Iron Age Britain and the near Continent exhibit clear archaeological reference to the centrality of feasting in the disposal of the dead. By no means universal across time zones or geographical areas, there is nonetheless a persistent vein of ritual involving pomp, ceremony and communal dining, albeit reserved for the rich and powerful in the community.

So what does such conspicuous consumption actually mean? Does the presence of eating and drinking equipment and the remains of butchered meat simply represent a jolly good send-off by convivial mourners consuming their 'baked meats'? Or does this material evidence for death-feasting have a deeper meaning, in terms of recognition of an afterlife? Was the role of the funerary feast to share a meal not only among mourners but also with the gods? Was the provision of food and drink seen as necessary for the dead person to be welcomed into the Happy Otherworld? The placing of food in graves is probably multi-faceted but, above all, it represented a powerful belief in some kind of existence beyond the grave, on the one hand and, on the other, recognition of the need to propitiate the spirit-guardians of the Otherworld.

• HEROIC DEATHS •

To the Celtiberians death in battle is glorious; and they consider it a crime to burn the body of such a warrior; for they believe that the soul goes up to the gods in heaven, if the body is devoured on the field by the hungry vulture.
SILIUS ITALICUS, *PUNICA* III, 342–48

Two Roman writers – Aelian and Silius Italicus – commented on a curious rite practised by the Celtiberians of northeast Spain. The bodies of noble warriors slain in battle were treated to excarnation

A Noble British Burial

In 1965, excavators of a gas pipe trench for a new housing development in Welwyn Garden City in southeast England came across a rich 2,000-year-old grave. It belonged to someone of the highest rank in late Iron Age British society, who died towards the end of the 1st century BC. Although some of the grave goods were smashed by the modern diggers, enough remained to allow archaeologists to piece together a reconstruction of the tomb. Against one wall stood six large Mediterranean wine amphorae, presumably once full to the brim. Resting on the floor were 36 fineware pots, mainly locally made but including two plates and a wine flagon imported from Gaul. Added to the wine paraphernalia were a silver goblet and a strainer to catch the sediment from the heavy red Italian wine.

The corpse had been wrapped in a bearskin before being cremated, for burnt claws survived in the grave. Next to the human remains was a set of 24 superb glass counters for use in a board game. One possible analogy is with the ancient Egyptian funerary game of *senet*: the presence of these counters might represent a game between the dead person and the spirits of the Otherworld. Perhaps the deceased had to win in order to gain access to the afterlife.

Late Iron Age noble burial, with feasting equipment, at Welwyn, Hertfordshire.

(the exposure of the corpse in the open air), in order for their flesh to be consumed by vultures. It was believed that these birds were sacred to the sky-god and that, in this manner, the souls of the valiant would be transported up to the gods in heaven.

In their epic poems the *Iliad* and the *Aeneid*, Homer and Virgil each described the funerary customs of the ancient Greeks and Trojans and the rites accorded those who had died bravely in battle. The disposal of these heroes was by cremation on huge funeral pyres, so that the remains would rise up to the sky and join the gods. Analogies to these burial rituals can be identified among the Britons around the time of the Roman conquest. In about AD 50 a chieftain died at Verulamium (St Albans). He lay in state for some time; he was placed on a funeral pyre, along with several of his belongings, and burnt. His remains were then placed in a tomb surrounded by an enclosure, at whose entrance the bodies of two women were interred, perhaps as spiritual guardians of the dead man. The burial-place, at Folly Lane to the north of the Iron Age and Roman city, remained a focal point throughout the Roman period, as if the memory of this noble Briton, as a kind of benevolent ancestor-god, somehow encompassed the very essence of the place.

Other distinctive burials of the later Iron Age in Britain may provide a window on infernal belief systems among the early Celts. One is of especial interest, firstly because the dead 'hero' was female and, secondly, because the grave goods and the body itself convey a potent message associated with the colour red, so significant in Otherworld symbolism of Celtic mythology. The woman's burial was at Wetwang in East Yorkshire. When she died, at the age of about 35, she was buried with a two-wheeled ceremonial chariot that she might have used in battle, and this was placed inverted over her body. Mourners had laid joints of pork on her torso and a mirror on her shins.

So far, the burial fits into a well-known series of chariot-burials from this part of northeast England. But the grave goods, including the horse gear and her headdress, showed a unique preponderance of red coral, imported from the Mediterranean. What is more, forensic evidence from distorted facial bones revealed that this woman had lived her life bearing a disfiguring bright red growth near her nose. Far from being shunned, this woman's affliction perhaps marked her out as special, and the richness of her burial may indicate a high status. Perhaps this 'red lady' enjoyed a particular rank because she was perceived to emanate from the Otherworld.

• LIFE IN THE OTHERWORLD •

When Arawn led Pwyll to his Otherworld kingdom of Annwfn, access seemed easy, with no special barriers or gateways to be negotiated. Indeed, Arawn reassured Pwyll that he would encounter no hindrance to his realm. Irish myths reveal other perceptions about how the world of the spirits could be reached. Water – lakes or the ocean – provided access points; so did caves leading underground, and ancient burial-mounds, such as Newgrange. Certain islands were perceived as otherworld places. The home of the sea-god Manannán was the otherworldly Isle of Man.

The 7th-century tale *The Voyage of Bran* tells the story of a journey made by Bran and his followers to the Land of Women, the Isle of Apple Trees, a manifestation of the Happy Otherworld, after he was lured there by one of its beautiful goddesses. The tale is an example of the two-edged nature of this world beyond the grave. It was an ageless, timeless place where Bran and his men dwelt contentedly for a while, but then some of his followers grew homesick and wanted to set sail for Ireland. The women of the island warned them not to touch the land, but as they approached the shore one of the band, more eager for home than the rest, jumped out of the boat and waded through the sea. As soon as his feet touched the beach, he crumbled to dust, having aged instantly by three hundred years.

Clochans (dry-stone 'beehive huts') perched on Skellig Michael, a remote island eight miles off the coast of southwest Ireland.

This Otherworld was the Land of Forever Young (Tir na n'Og), but the enchantment ceased to work if humans returned to their own world of time. The name Avalon, the legendary island burial-place of King Arthur, means 'Apple Tree Island'. According to medieval French Arthurian Romances, such as the story of the Holy Grail, Avalon was situated at Glastonbury, an 'island' in the middle of the marshy, low-lying and apple-rich Somerset Levels.

Other legends, too, relate encounters between living people and the Otherworld. One story is about a man called Nera, who lived in Connacht when Queen Medbh and her consort Ailill were in power. Nera strayed into the Otherworld through an access-point at the Cave of Cruachain, a natural fissure in a limestone outcrop in Co. Roscommon, but identified in myth as a *sídh*. It happened at Samhain, the autumn festival between the old and new years, when the boundaries between the human and spirit worlds became unusually porous.

Although a live mortal and a trespasser into the land of the gods, Nera was permitted to stay and even to marry a goddess of the *sídh*. She prophesied that Medbh's royal court of Cruachain would be destroyed by fire unless the *sídh* itself were first ravaged. Nera returned to earthworld in the wintertime to warn Medbh, carrying unseasonal summer plants – primrose, garlic and golden fern – in order to prove to his people that he had come from the Otherworld, where time was different from that on earth. Connacht's forces invaded and looted the *sídh*, carrying off great treasures, but Nera remained with his wife and family, never to return to the world of humans.

• DOWN AMONG THE DEAD •

J. R. R. Tolkien in *The Lord of the Rings* paints several wonderful images of the dead. Perhaps the most striking is the journey of Sam and Frodo across the Dead Marshes on their way to Mordor, guided by the corrupted once-hobbit Gollum. This desolate expanse of marshland is lit with will-o'-the-wisp flames. Beneath the surface of the stagnant wetland, they can see the bodies of those who had died in battle with evil forces, perfectly preserved, their pale faces looking as though they were merely asleep. In the films, Frodo strays off the path and tumbles into the water, appearing to join the world of the dead who are eager to keep him in their realm under the surface.

Tolkein's imagery here resonates with archaeological findings of bog-bodies, the remains of humans who were for some reason placed in marshes during the Iron Age and Roman periods in Britain, Ireland and other parts of Northern Europe where raised bogs have formed. Many of these ancient bog-people display signs of violent and untimely death, often by garrotting or hanging. Why certain individuals were chosen to be disposed of in this way remains a mystery, but it must have something to do with the desire to

Oisin and the Land of Forever Young

The treachery of the Otherworld is displayed in a Fenian Cycle tale highly reminiscent of the *Voyage of Bran*. The Fenian chieftain Finn had a son, Oisin ('Young Deer'). One day, while out hunting, Finn's warband, the Fianna, met a beautiful young woman called Niav. Oisin fell in love with her and she tempted him away to her realm, the Happy Otherworld, a land of perpetual youth. While he dwelt there, time stood still, but at length he began to be homesick.

Niav reluctantly gave him leave to visit Ireland one last time but warned him on no account to touch his homeland with any part of his body. She lent him her white horse but, as Oisin reached Ireland, he saw that hundreds of years had gone by, leaving no trace of the Fianna. So shocked was he that he reined in his horse; in doing so, the girth broke, throwing Oisin onto the beach, where extreme old age caught up with him and he crumbled to dust.

Late Iron Age bronze stag from Neuvy-en-Sullias, Loiret, France.

interrupt the normal process of bodily decay and, perhaps therefore, to 'freeze-frame' it halfway between the material and other worlds.

It may have been deemed important for the person not to proceed to become an ancestor-spirit because of some conduct or status when alive. It could have been for a negative reason, because the deceased's spirit was too dangerous to let loose in the afterlife, or a positive one, the perceived necessity to keep the individual 'on tap' to continue helping the living community, maybe because he or she had been a powerful and useful go-between, able to connect the world of humans with that of the gods.

Two Irish bog-bodies were those of men who died in about 300 BC, and they were discovered in 2003 by peat-workers in Co. Offaly and Co. Meath. The inference that they were special people rests on their physical characteristics and their places of discovery in locations identified as medieval land-boundaries (which might have had much earlier origins). One of those found, Oldcroghan Man, was an enormous 1.91 m (6ft 4 in.) tall and built to match; his status is suggested by his unique plaited leather armband inlaid with decorated metal. The second, Clonycavan Man, was slightly built and much shorter. The feature that made him distinctive was the arrangement of his long hair in a complex style on top of his head, kept in place by a kind of hair gel made from animal fat and pine resin imported from southern France or Spain. This must have been a costly cosmetic and either conferred or acknowledged Clonycavan Man's status. The presence of parasites in the hair indicate that he had kept it up and gelled for some time before death, so the elaborate hairstyle was not part of a corpse-dressing ritual.

Both individuals had been subjected to sustained and brutal injuries that ultimately led to their horrific deaths. Oldcroghan's arms were pierced through with twisted hazel ropes; his nipples were sliced through just as he died; finally he was beheaded and chopped in half. Clonycavan was disembowelled and sustained a frenzied rain of axe-blows to his head. These men must have occupied a special place in life and underwent special deaths. Their burial in peat bogs on boundaries may indicate their careful disposal at perceived gateways to the Otherworld. They may have been sacrificed because of crimes or the breaking of taboos, or simply because they were special people, even shamans, who were too dangerous (and maybe too valuable) to be allowed normal death and burial.

Lindow Man

In August 1984, the mechanical digger of peat-cutters working at Lindow Moss in Cheshire uncovered a human arm, part of a 2,000-year-old bog-body. The remains were those of a young man in his prime, about 25 years old. He was naked but for an armlet made of fox-fur, and no grave goods accompanied him. The mistletoe in his digested food revealed that he had eaten a special 'last supper'. Like the Irish victims, this man had horrific injuries leading to his death: most significant were at least two blows to the head that cracked his skull and stunned him; he was then garrotted and, at the same time, his throat was cut.

The triple manner of his death has led some to connect him with the early medieval myth of the ritual threefold death that befell some Irish kings. One of these was the 6th-century AD Diarmaid mac Cerbhaill, who enquired of his wise men the manner of his death. The answer was that he would be stabbed, drowned in a vat of ale and burnt. Diarmaid scorned the prophecy, but it came to pass. Lindow Man was selected for a special death and burial. It was important that his body would be frozen in time, not permitted to decay, so the normal rites of death and ease of passage to the next world were denied him. His journey to the Otherworld was halted at the gate leading out from the world of humans.

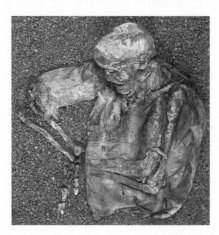

Lindow Man, the late Iron Age body found in a peat bog at Lindow Moss, Cheshire.

• THE AMBIGUITY OF THE CELTIC OTHERWORLD •

It is not easy to grasp the concept of the Celtic world of the dead. Chimaera-like, the images of the afterlife seem constantly to shift and change, according to what kind of evidence is considered. The Otherworld could be up in the sky, down below ground, in a cave or on an island. Unlike the world of humans, earthly time had no meaning there. The mythic literature presents a capricious, fickle Otherworld that was both wonderful and awful. In Irish tradition, the spirits meddled constantly with living humans, for good or evil, depending on their caprice. Entrances to the Otherworld were liminal places, fraught with peril and menace. But, at the same time, the afterlife is presented as a marvellous land, flowing with treasure and sumptuous feasts, where nobody grew old. Welsh myths paint a similar, though more muted, story.

In both Ireland and Wales, the Otherworld was uncomfortably close to earthly life. Portents and magical symbols proclaimed its propinquity to living people. Above all, though, both medieval traditions told only of noble families and their experiences with the spirit world. For endorsement by archaeological evidence, it is necessary to consult the material culture of the pre-Roman Iron Age, and that of course presents problems of chronology. Can we assume that the deposition in water of ancient cauldrons has any bearing on the nature of magical cauldrons of rebirth that lurks within Irish and Welsh mythology? Does the lavish evidence for funerary feasts in rich Iron Age tombs have any connections with the banquets of the Irish *sídhe*? If the links have any genuine validity, how did the traditions of the late 1st century BC percolate through to the storytellers and monastic scribes of medieval times? Like the Otherworld itself, these are slippery issues and definitive answers may never be found.

PAGANISM AND CHRISTIANITY: THE TRANSFORMATION OF MYTH

This is the penitence of a Druid or a cruel man vowed to evil,
or a satirist or a cohabiter or a heretic or an adulterer, namely
seven years on bread and water.

FROM A 7TH-CENTURY IRISH PENITENTIAL

The *Altram Tige dá Medar* is an Irish late medieval text that records a direct challenge of paganism by the Christian faith. Oenghus, god of lovers and Manannán, god of the sea, belong to the divine race the Tuatha Dé Danann. But in the text, both gods admitted that the Christian God possesses far greater power than any of the pagan Irish divinities.

As early as the 7th century AD, Irish stories were written that contained juxtapositions between paganism and Christianity, in which the latter inevitably triumphed. Brigit was both a goddess and a Christian saint. In her pagan persona, she was a member of the Tuatha Dé Danann, and was both a single and a triple deity. She had a wide range of functions, including craftworking, healing (particularly in relation to women in childbirth) and poetry; she was also patron of dairies and ale-brewing. Her festival was at Imbolc, when the birth of new lambs was celebrated.

I am unclean but that girl is full of the Holy Spirit.
However, she does not take my food.

FROM THE *VITA BRIGITAE*

Brigit is a rare example of a Celtic goddess who exists also as a Christian saint. In the 7th century AD, a monk called Cogitosus wrote a biography of St Brigit in Latin, the *Vita Brigitae*. This holy woman is alleged to have been the founder-abbess of a Christian monastery at Kildare in the 5th or 6th century, but she may belong to legend rather than reality. The treatment of Brigit in the early texts displays a wonderful amalgam of pagan and Christian elements that plays out the tension when the two systems confronted each other. Brigit was reared in a Druid's household and, since she could not stomach the food he gave her because it was tainted by a pagan hand, she was fed the milk of a special white red-eared cow – its colours proclaiming it as belonging to the pagan Otherworld. Brigit's Druid foster-father recognized her purity and warmed to the Christian religion. He even chose her name (that of an Irish goddess) after three Christian monks appeared to him in a dream and instructed him to call her Brigit. But even as a Christian holy woman, she retained some of her pagan responsibilities, particularly butter-making and brewing.

While the story of Brigit presents the adoption of Christianity over paganism as a peaceful and virtually seamless transition, the same is certainly not true of the 7th-century sources for the life of Saint Patrick, who was credited with having converted Ireland to Christianity in AD 432. His stories are shot through with episodes of conflict between pagans and Christians. In particular, Patrick is credited with challenging the supremacy and magical powers of the court Druids, the king's advisors, who bitterly resented Patrick's scornful dismissal of their spiritual abilities. One especially powerful story concerns the Christian saint's feud with Lucat, King Loeghaire's Druid. He attempted to poison Patrick's wine at Tara during a major pagan religious festival and, when he failed, Lucat then challenged him to a trial by fire, which Patrick won. Loeghaire was convinced of Patrick's superior power and converted to Christianity.

The written evidence for Brigit and Patrick is literary testament to the interface between Christianity and paganism in the mid-1st millennium AD, represented by Druids and saints. But other evidence also points to connections between the old polytheistic systems and the new monotheism. The Trinitarian nature

19th-century stained-glass window depicting Saint Brigit, Ballylynan, Co. Laois, Ireland.

of Christianity – the Father, Son and Holy Spirit – resonated well with the established triadism of Celtic paganism. The myths (and earlier cult-symbols) are bristling with triple imagery, so three-ness was a comfortable and familiar concept that could be used by Christian missionaries to gain currency with the pagan mind.

The transition between paganism and Christianity can be mapped not only in literature but also in art. There is a 19th-century stone carving in Llandaff Cathedral, Cardiff, that depicts a triple head, symbol of the Trinity, that would be perfectly at home as an image of a pagan mythic triple head. The idea of using aspects of pagan belief as conduits in conversion can be seen in archaeological evidence belonging to the Constantinian period of the 4th century AD. In 1975, a hoard of early Christian church plate was discovered by a metal-detectorist at the Roman town of Durobrivae in Cambridgeshire. Among the pieces were silver feather-shaped plaques, familiar votive objects deposited in pagan Romano-British shrines. But these were decorated in gold with the Chi–Rho monogram, a symbol made up of the first two Greek letters of the word Christ. Surely these objects were carefully used to re-package the symbolism of an old faith-system to win over hearts and minds to the new.

The human head is another persistent theme in both the myths and pre-Christian imagery. But early Christian artists, too, were fascinated by this religious icon. Heads of exaggerated size appear on 8th–9th-century Irish crosses, like those of the Apostles clustered around the base of the Cross of Moone in Co. Kildare, and of Christ on the coeval crucifixion plaque from Rinnagan, near Athlone. Perhaps the most evocative piece of Christian Celtic art is on one of the illuminated manuscripts, the wonderful Chi–Rho page from the late 8th/early 9th-century Book of Kells. The page is covered in patterns, including countless triskeles (a three-armed whirligig beloved of Iron Age metalsmiths in Ireland and Wales). But dominating the page is a disembodied human head.

When the Emperor Constantine declared Christianity to be the state religion of Rome in the early 4th century AD, paganism – whether Celtic or Roman – certainly did not vanish overnight, but continued for centuries. The Celtic myths, compiled in writing by monks, but drawing upon the much earlier oral repertoire of storytellers, enshrined a pagan tradition that, despite being manipulated by its Christian scribes, trawled deep into its past. Some of the monks responsible for writing down the myths may even have been brought up in the milieu of oral storytelling. Whether or not that was the case, and despite the Christian gloss that can sometimes be observed, the vernacular myths of Ireland and Wales have been preserved, to chronicle or create a rich and colourful tapestry of ancient gods, supernatural creatures, enchantments, and tales of the constant interference of the spirits in human affairs. The power of the pagan mythic tradition continued to manifest itself centuries after Christianity was commonplace in Celtic lands, and was by no means obliterated by the new monotheistic faith: people living in the later 1st millennium AD may well have been public Christians and private pagans.

General and translations

Davies, S., trans., *The Mabinogion. The Great Medieval Celtic Tales*, Oxford, 2007

Delaney, F., *Legends of the Celts*, London, 1989

Gantz, J., trans., *Early Irish Myths and Sagas*, London, 1981

Green, M. J., *Dictionary of Celtic Myth and Legend*, London and New York, 1992

Green, M. J., *Celtic Myths*, London, 1993

Green, M. J., ed., *The Celtic World*, London and New York, 1995

Green, M. J., and R. Howell, *Pocket Guide to Celtic Wales*, Cardiff, 2000

James, S., *Exploring the World of the Celts*, London and New York, 1993

Kinsella, T., trans., *The Táin*, Oxford, 1969

Mac Cana, P., *Celtic Mythology*, Feltham, England, 1983

O'Faolain, E., *Irish Sagas and Folk-Tales*, Oxford, 1954

Druids

Aldhouse-Green, M. J., *Caesar's Druids*, New Haven and London, 2010

Chadwick, N., *The Druids*, Cardiff, 1997 (2nd edn; 1st edn 1966)

Cunliffe, B., *Druids. A Very Short Introduction*, Oxford, 2010

Fitzpatrick, A. P., *Who Were The Druids?*, London, 1997

Green, M. J., *Exploring the World of the Druids*, London and New York, 1997

Archaeology

Brunaux, J.-L., trans. D. Nash, *The Celtic Gauls: Gods, Rites and Sanctuaries*, London, 1988

Green, M. J., *The Gods of the Celts*, Stroud, 1986

Raftery, B., *Pagan Celtic Ireland*. London and New York, 1994

The Celtic Debate

Collis, J., *The Celts. Origins, Myths, Inventions*, Stroud, 2003

James, S., *The Atlantic Celts. Ancient People or Modern Invention?*, London, 1999

Volumes not included above are as follows:

Caldecott, M., *Women in Celtic Myth*, London, 1988

Carson, C., *The Tain: A New Translation of the Táin Bó Cúailnge*, London 2008

Duff, E., trans. *Silius Italicus Punica*, London, 1949

Falconer, W., trans., *Cicero de Divinatione*, London, 1922

Graves, R., trans., *Lucan Pharsalia*, Harmondsworth, 1956

Harrison, G. B., (ed.), *Macbeth: The Penguin Shakespeare*, Harmondsworth, 1937

Hennessey, W. M., 'The ancient Irish Goddess of War', *Revue Celtique* 1, 1870–72

Jones, G., and T. Jones, *The Mabinogion*, London, 1974

Minahane, J., *The Christian Druids. On the Filid or Philosopher-Poets of Ireland*, Dublin, 1993

O'Faoláin, E., *Irish Sagas and Folk Tales*, Dublin, 1986

Ross, A., *Pagan Celtic Britain*, London, 1967

Sjöblom, T., 'Advice from a Birdman: Ritual Injunctions and Royal Instruction in TBDD', in A. Ahlqvist, G. W. Banks, R. Latvio, H. Nyberg and T. Sjöblom, eds, *Celtica Helsingensia*, Helsinki, 1996, 233–51

Stokes, W., *Coir Anman*, Leipzig, 1897

Thorpe, L., trans., *Giraldus Cambrensis. The Journey Through Wales*, Harmondsworth, 1978

Tierney, J. J., 'The Celtic Ethnography of Posidonius', *Proceedings of the Royal Irish Academy* 60, 247–75

Webb, J. F., trans., *Navigatio Brendani. The Voyage of Saint Brendan*, Harmondsworth, 1965

Webb, T., ed., *W.B Yeats Selected Poems*, London, 2000

Winterbottom, M., *The Ruin of Britain and Other Works*, London, 1978

Wiseman, A., and P. Wiseman, trans., *Julius Caesar. The Battle for Gaul*, London, 1980

Sources for individual quotations

7   W. B. Yeats *Cuchulain's Fight with the Sea*, lines 75–83; Webb (T.) 2000, 26

10   Wiseman and Wiseman 1980, 17

15   Jones and Jones 1974, 43

16   Raftery 1994, 98

20   Davies 2007, 48

22   Kinsella 1969, 48–9

25   Jones and Jones 1974, 30

30   Kinsella 1969, 37

34   Sjöblom 1996, 236

38   Wiseman and Wiseman 1980, 121

40a   Davies 2007, 68

40b   Wiseman and Wiseman 1980, 12

42   Cicero *de Divinatione*; Falconer 1922

45   Kinsella 1969, 3, 9

48   Voyage of St Brendan; Webb (J. F.) 1965, 35–6

49   Gildas *de Excidio Britanniae* 4, 2–3; Winterbottom 1978, 17

50   Giraldus Cambrensis; Thorpe 1978, 114

54   Davies 2007, 10

56   Green 1997, 153

58   Kinsella 1969, 98

59   Delaney 1989, 3

61   O'Faoláin 1986, 3

62   Gantz 1981, 39

70   Delaney 1989, 58

72   Green 1997, 129

77   Davies 2007, 8

81   Davies 2007, 9 (with slight change by author)

84   Davies 2007, 47

86   Jones and Jones 1974, 46–7

93   Jones and Jones 1974, 10

95   Jones and Jones 1974, 184–5

98   Tierney 1959–60, 247

101   Gantz 1981, 182

104   Kinsella 1969, 62

105   Kinsella 1969, 84

108   Kinsella 1969, 150

109   Kinsella 1969, 85

112   Davies 2007, 18

116   Davies 2007, 204

117   Davies 2007, 52

118   Kinsella 1969, 29

121   Kinsella 1969, 133

123   Ross 1967, 100; after Stokes 1897, 384, para 241

126   Gantz 1981, 66 (with minor author changes)

129   Davies 2007, 180

130   Kinsella 1969, 49

136   Jones and Jones 1974, 70

138   Caldecott 1988, 4

139   Shakespeare, *Macbeth* Act 1, Scene 3; Harrison ed. 1937, 23

140   Kinsella 1969, 126

142   Kinsella 1969, 7

145   Carson 2008, 12

146   Gantz 1981, 76

147   Hennessey 1870–2, 37

149   Davies 2007, 29 (modified by author)

150   Jones and Jones 1974, 63

156a   Kinsella 1969, 30

156b   Lucan *Pharsalia*; Graves 1956, 78–9

159   Davies 2007, 62

161   Delaney 1989, 85

164   O'Faoláin 1986, 31

168   O'Faoláin 1986, 23

172   Kinsella 1969, 27

176   O'Faoláin 1986, 164

178   Davies 2007, 3

181   Graves 1956, 38

182   Davies 2007, 25

185   Gantz 1981, 180

186   Wiseman and Wiseman 1980, 124

187   Duff 1949, 139

197a   Green 1997, 134, after Minahane 1993

197b   Green 1997, 136, after Minahane 1993

a = above, b = below, l = left, r = right

1 Photo Jean Roubier; 2 Paul Jenkins; 8, 9 Martin Lubikowski, ML Design, London; 13 Humber Archaeological Partnership, Hull; 16 © National Monuments Service, Dublin. Department of Arts, Heritage and the Gaeltacht; 18l Royal Irish Academy, Dublin; 18r Jesus College, Oxford; 20 Ulster Museum, Belfast; 21 Newport Museum & Art Gallery; 23 Illustration © Anne Leaver; 28, 29 Nationalmuseet, Denmark; 31 Corinium Museum, Cirencester; 32 National Museum of Ireland, Dublin; 35 Paul Jenkins; 41 Musée Historique et Archéologique, Orléans; 43 Paul Jenkins; 45 National Gallery of Scotland, Edinburgh; 47 Paul Jenkins; 51 Universitätsbibliothek, Heidelberg/Bridgeman Art Library; 52 Rheinisches Landesmuseum, Stuttgart; 55 British Museum, London; 60 The Irish Times; 63 Photo: Carole Raddato; 64 Paul Jenkins; 65 Bristol City Museum; 71 Gloucester City Museum; 72 Paul Jenkins; 75 The Irish Times; 78 Paul Jenkins; 79 Nationalmuseet, Denmark; 89a Landesmuseum, Zurich; 89b National Museum of Ireland, Dublin; 94 Barbara Crow; 97 © Crown Copyright (2014) Visit Wales; 100 National Museum of Ireland, Dublin; 102 Musée d'Archéologie Nationale, St-Germain-en-Laye; 107 TopFoto; 109 Werner Forman/Corbis; 111 Irish Tourist Board; 113 Musée Historique et Archéologique, Orléans; 114 Paul Jenkins; 115 Miranda Aldhouse-Green; 120 Musée de la Préhistoire Finistérienne, Brittany; 121 The Trustees of the British Museum, London; 122 Nationalmuseet, Denmark; 123 National Museum of Wales, Cardiff; 124 Musée National du Moyen Âge, Paris; 127 Illustration © Anne Leaver; 128 Musée Archéologique, Dijon; 132 Musée National du Moyen Âge, Paris; 134 National Museum of Wales, Cardiff; 136 Miranda Aldhouse-Green; 140 Nationalmuseet, Denmark; 142 Stephen Conlin; 143 Paul Jenkins; 144, 147 Miranda Aldhouse-Green; 148 Illustration Rowena Alsey; 152 Newport Museum & Art Gallery; 153 Archäologiemuseum, Graz; 155 Musée de Bretagne, Rennes; 157 from William Stukeley, *Stonehenge, a Temple Restor'd to the British Druids, 1740*; 162 Musée Archéologique, Dijon/ Bridgeman Art Library; 163 National Museum of Ireland, Dublin; 165 Peter Zoeller/Design Pics/Corbis; 166 Miranda Aldhouse-Green; 169 The Irish Times; 170 Department of Defence, Dublin; 172 National Geographic Image Collection/Alamy; 174 Miranda Aldhouse-Green; 177 Paul Jenkins; 179 Miranda Aldhouse-Green; 183 Nationalmuseet, Denmark; 184 National Museum of Wales, Cardiff; 186 Paul Sampson/Travel/Alamy; 188 The Trustees of the British Museum, London; 191 Tom Bean/Corbis; 193 Musée Historique et Archéologique, Orléans; 195 The Trustees of the British Museum, London; 199 Irish Tourist Board.